Oxford Heritage W

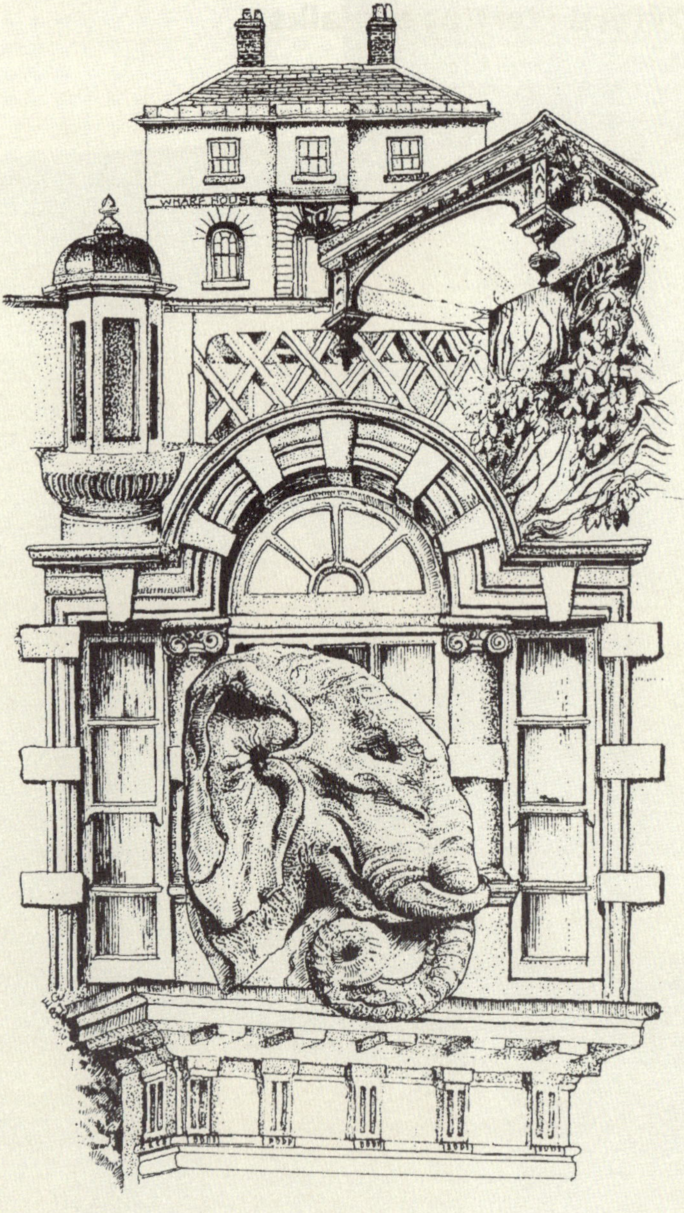
WHARF HOUSE

Oxford Heritage Walks
On foot from Carfax to Turn Again

Malcolm Graham
Illustrated by Edith Gollnast
Cartography by Alun Jones

OXFORD
PRESERVATION
TRUST

Oxford Preservation Trust

www.oxfordpreservation.org.uk

First published in Great Britain 2019

Illustrations produced by Edith Gollnast
Map produced by Alun Jones
Frontispiece by Edith Gollnast
Designed by Nick Clarke

Copyright © Oxford Preservation Trust 2019

All rights reserved. No parts of this work may be reproduced, stored in a retrieval system, or transmitted, in any form or by an means, electronic, mechanical, photocopying, recording or otherwise, without the prior permission of the publishers.

A catalogue of this book is available from the British Library
ISBN 978-0-9576797-6-4

Printed and bound at Holywell Press, Oxford

ALSO IN THE OXFORD HERITAGE WALKS SERIES

Book1: On foot from Oxford Castle to St Giles'

Book 2: On foot from Broad Street

Book 3: On foot from Catte Street to Parson's Pleasure

Book 4: On foot from Paradise Street to Sheepwash

Contents

About Oxford Preservation Trust   page 7

Table of Illustrations   page 9

Foreword   page 11

WALKS

1 Carfax to St Ebbe's Church   page 17

2 Pembroke Street to Christ Church   page 27

3 Brewer Street to Clark's Row   page 37

4 The Friars and St Ebbe's   page 49

5 Oxford Castle and Paradise   page 61

About Oxford Preservation Trust

Oxford Preservation Trust is a well-established and forward-thinking charity which owns, restores and cares for land and buildings in the City, its setting and its views. A significant part of our work is in providing public open access, not least through the success of our project Oxford Open Doors, and in sharing and encouraging an interest in the City and its history.

Throughout its history Oxford has changed and expanded, and throughout the life of the Trust this has been accepted and embraced. Our work is to guide that change and not to stop it. Sir Michael Sadler, founder Trustee, states in the Trust's First Annual Report in 1927:

"Oxford is growing. Its growth may be guided but should not be grudged. The work of the Trust is not to hamper Oxford but to help it. The beauty of Oxford is one of the treasures of the world."

Sir Michael Sadler, founder Trustee, OPT Annual Report (1927)

This guide records some of the changes that have happened within our beautiful city. It fills in some of the gaps, and records some of the lost buildings and memories, building up a picture and helping to make sense of Oxford's rich history, so that it can be better appreciated and enjoyed, now and in the future. These series of books are a reminder of the contribution more modest buildings and features make to our enjoyment of the streetscapes and skyline and of their importance to the city.

We are delighted that these Heritage Walks will enable a new audience to get to know and appreciate more about Oxford. Debbie Dance, Director, 2019

Oxford Preservation Trust thanks the Greening Lamborn Trust, CPRE Oxfordshire Buildings Preservation Trust, the Barnsbury Charitable Trust, Mrs Margaret Leighfield and the William Delafield Charitable Trust for their generous donations to this project. We record our gratitude to Alun Jones, who died in 2018, leaving behind his characterful maps for us to use, and to John Ashdown for his architectural and historical advice.

The Greening Lamborn Trust's objective is to promote public interest in the history, architecture, old photographs and heraldry of Oxford and its neighbourhood by supporting publications and other media that create access to them.

Table of Illustrations

1 Carfax to St Ebbe's Church
1. St Scholastica's Day plaque, Abbey House
2. Butter Bench, Carfax, mid 18th century view
3. 36–37 Queen Street
4. 17th century building, corner of St Ebbe's Street, (demolished)
5. Donkey advertising Cape's store
6. Cartouche, Royal Blenheim pub
7. West door, St Ebbe's Church

2 Pembroke Street to Christ Church
8. View over gables of Royal Blenheim pub to tower of former City Brewery
9. Royal arms of Queen Victoria, 20 Pembroke Street
10. Lanterns, Oxford Story Museum
11. View through iron gates of Beef Lane and Besse Building, Pembroke College
12. Figurative panels on 1961 extension to St Aldate's Church
13. Oriel window, Pembroke College
14. Christ Church almshouses, from a sketch c.1830
15. Carved stone putti, Christ Church

3 Brewer Street to Clark's Row
16. Campion Hall with part of Christ Church Cathedral School on left, Brewer Street
17. Littlegate from a sketch by John Malchair, 1785
18. Victorian Drinking Fountain, now removed
19. Trill Mill Stream in Littlegate Street, from a sketch by B. C. Buckler, c.1820
20. Carved brackets, Bishop King's Palace
21. Post medieval wooden shutter
22. Littlemore Court from a photograph by Henry Minn, 1910

4 The Friars and St Ebbe's
23. A Blackfriar (not shown on map)
24. Shop in Commercial Road from an old photograph (demolished)
25. 8–10 Turn Again Lane
26. A group of Greyfriars (not shown on map)

5 Oxford Castle and Paradise

27. 29a Castle Street
28. Detail of Greyfriars cartouche, Paradise House
29. Metal swallows on timber footbridge near Empress Court
30. Empress Matilda's door in St George's Tower
31. King Stephen and Empress Matilda puppets
32. Lloyd's Bank weathervane, 1–3 High Street

Foreword

This book is the fifth in the series Oxford Heritage Walks which revisits and expands upon the On Foot in Oxford leaflets and booklets published by Oxford City Libraries and Oxfordshire County Libraries between 1973 and 1988. Twelve of these trails were published in all, two of them being subsequently revised and reissued under variant titles. They were written by Malcolm Graham, Local Studies Librarian for Oxford City until 1974 and for Oxfordshire from 1974. Local artists supplied the drawings, Laura Potter illustrating the first eight trails and Edith Gollnast the others. Oxford Preservation Trust gratefully acknowledges copyright permission from Oxfordshire County Council to reuse text and illustrations from these publications.

Like the earlier trails, the Oxford Heritage Walks hope to encourage interest in the history of the City and the evolution of the built environment. They are not primarily guides to Oxford's world-famous architectural treasures for which there are many alternative sources. Rather, they explore how each area has developed and focus attention on the streets and buildings of local importance which add character to every corner of our City. They contain a treasure-chest of information about Oxford and a veritable arsenal of historical evidence with which to defend those features which make the City a special place.

About Oxford Heritage Walks

Author

Malcolm Graham read History at Nottingham University before doing a postgraduate librarianship course in Leeds and an MA in English Local History at Leicester University. He came to Oxford in 1970 as the City's first full-time local history librarian and took on the same role for the County in 1974. Between 1991 and 2008, he was Head of Oxfordshire Studies with Oxfordshire County Council. He has published extensively on local history – his first On Foot in Oxford town trail appeared in 1973 – and he has given hundreds of talks and broadcasts over the years. He was awarded a PhD by Leicester University for a study of the development of Oxford's Victorian suburbs and he is a Fellow of the Society of Antiquaries of London. Away from local history, he enjoys walking, cycling, outdoor swimming, music and the theatre. He is married and lives in Botley.

Illustrator

Edith Gollnast studied art and design at Banbury School of Art and architectural conservation at Bristol University. For thirty five years she worked with historic buildings and areas at Oxford City Council. Edith lives in Oxford, where she enjoys creative activities, the arts and walking.

Cartographer

Alun Jones (1927-2018) was a Cartographer who created clear handwritten maps, often combining historical information and topography. His Classics degree was followed by the Diploma in Classical Archaeology at Oxford University in 1952; his fieldwork involved training in photography, Land Survey and technical drawing (using the traditional instruments of pre-digital recording). The history and practice of letters and writing, cartography, calligraphy and printing and book production were major interests while on the Staff of the Printer to the University (Oxford University Press) and then at the Alden Press, Oxford (1958-1982). Alun was later appointed Dean of the Centre for Medieval Studies, Oxford. Many of his maps were made for Oxford Preservation Trust, CPRE Oxfordshire and the Garden History Society as a service to the community. In 2001 he was elected a Fellow of the British Cartographic Society. Alun died in 2018, but will live on through his maps.

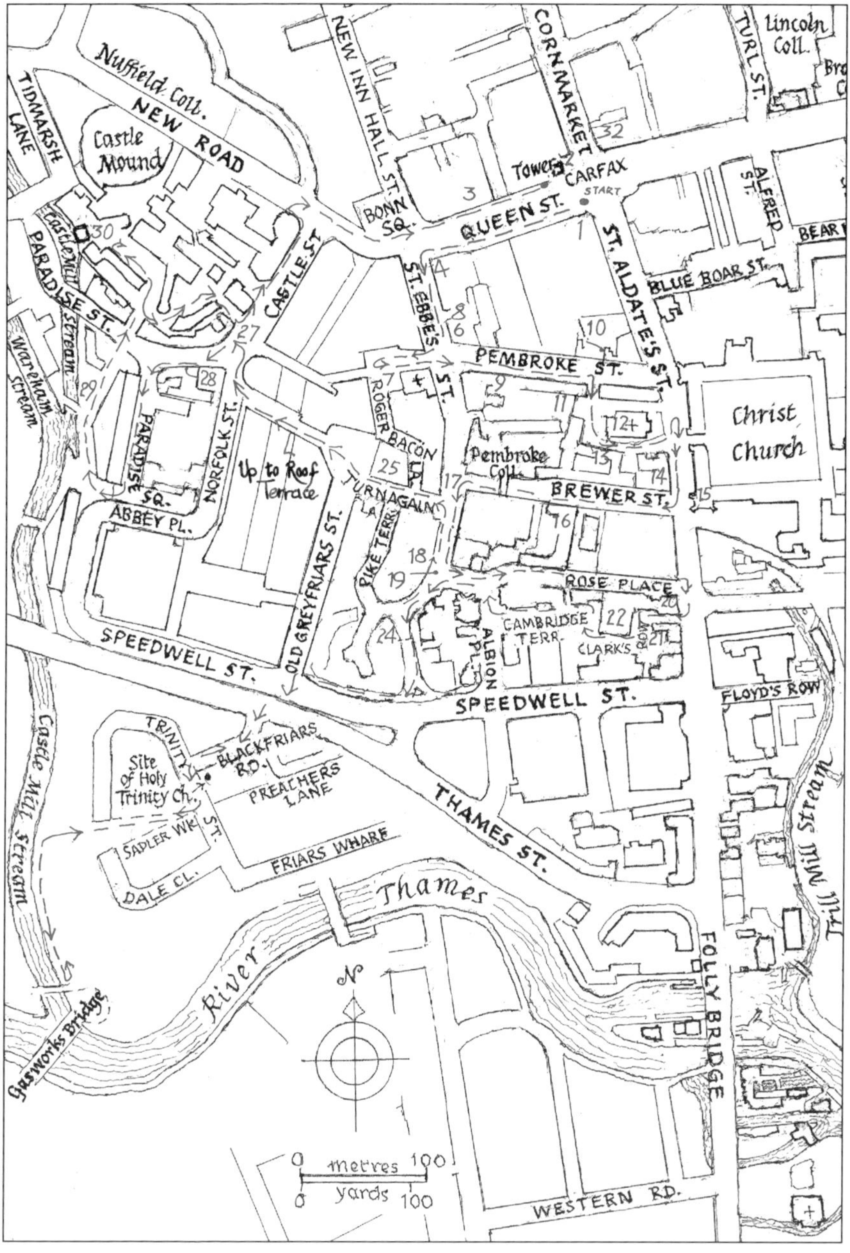
Nuffield Coll.
NEW ROAD
Castle Mound
TIDMARSH LANE
NEW INN HALL ST.
CORNMARKET
TURL ST.
Lincoln Coll.
Tower
CARFAX
START
BONN SQ.
QUEEN ST.
ALFRED ST.
BEAR
BLUE BOAR ST.
ST. ALDATE'S ST.
CASTLE ST.
PARADISE ST.
Castle Mill Stream
Wareham Stream
ST. EBBE'S ST.
PEMBROKE ST.
ROGER BACON LA.
Pembroke Coll.
Christ Church
BREWER ST.
PARADISE SQ.
NORFOLK ST.
Up to Roof Terrace
TURNAGAIN LA.
ABBEY PL.
OLD GREYFRIARS ST.
PIKE TERR.
ROSE PLACE
CAMBRIDGE TERR.
CLARK'S ROW
ALBION PL.
SPEEDWELL ST.
FLOYD'S ROW
TRINITY ST.
BLACKFRIARS RD.
Site of Holy Trinity Ch.
PREACHERS LANE
THAMES ST.
SADLER WK.
FRIARS WHARF
DALE CL.
Castle Mill Stream
Thames
River
Trill Mill Stream
FOLLY BRIDGE
Gasworks Bridge
N
metres
yards
WESTERN RD.

1 Carfax to St Ebbe's Church

Carfax takes its name from the Latin 'quadrifurcus' (four-forked) or the Norman French 'quatre vois' (four ways). The crossroads lay at the heart of the late-Saxon planned town laid out in c.900, and metaphorically at least it still fulfils this function for today's Greater Oxford. The development of Carfax was described in detail in *Oxford Heritage Walks Book 2, Oxford from Broad Street*, but some historical context will be useful before you head into Queen Street. Carfax today is the product of extensive widening and re-modelling between the 1890s and the early 1930s. Carfax Tower, restored and altered (1897, T. G. Jackson) is, in essence, the 14th century tower of the former City Church of St Martin, first recorded in 1032. The rest of the church, rebuilt in 1821–2, was demolished in 1896. Notice Tower House (1896), beside Carfax Tower, which was designed by H. T. Hare, architect of Oxford's newly-built Town Hall. Hare also designed the HSBC bank building (1896), originally Frank East's drapery store, on the Cornmarket Street corner, but the City rejected his proposal to turn Carfax Tower into an ornate clock tower in favour of Jackson's more conservative approach. The north-east corner of Carfax was widened a few years later, making space for the riotously ornamental Lloyds Bank (1900–3, Stephen Salter).

Carfax was at the heart of Oxford's street markets from medieval times until 1773–4 when traders were moved into the new Covered Market. The highly decorative Carfax Conduit (1616–17, John Clark) was placed in this central space as part of a scheme to bring spring water into the City from North Hinksey. It was removed as an obstruction to traffic in 1787, and was re-erected as an ornament in Nuneham Park where it still remains.

During the 1920s, Carfax became the crossroads for increasingly busy major roads which were now designated as the A34 and the A40, and the southern corners were widened and rebuilt in a chaste municipal style (1930–1, Ashley & Newman). Abbey House, on the south-west corner, incorporates the site of Oxford's first town hall, in use until 1229, which fronted Queen Street opposite St Martin's Church. Note the plaque beside the main entrance recalling the riot that began at the Swindlestock Tavern (c.1279–1709) on this site on St Scholastica's Day, February 10th, 1355. A dispute between a group of scholars and the landlord over the quality of his wine escalated into a three-day battle between Town and Gown. The King subsequently gave the University considerable power over the day-to-day running of the City, and Oxford's leading citizens were obliged every St Scholastica's Day to attend the University Church and do penance for the misdeeds of their predecessors. This humiliating ceremony continued in modified form until 1859.

A colonnaded Butter Bench was built on the site of the Swindlestock Tavern in c.1709, linked to Nicholas Hawksmoor's grander scheme for a civic forum. The underground vault where trouble began in 1355 was retained, and later became part of an extensive network of wine cellars extending across St Aldate's, and along the south side of High Street. Butter sellers were relocated to the Covered Market in 1781, and part of the Butter Bench was adapted (c.1840) for use as the City's first police station. Boffin's half-timbered baker's shop and first-floor café (1871, F. J. Codd) occupied the site until 1930 when both that building and the medieval cellars beneath were destroyed. Abbey House set a new building line for the south side of Queen Street but this was never implemented, as shown by the protruding stone-fronted building next door (2017, Wright & Wright) which forms part of a mixed development for Christ Church, providing

THIS WAS THE SITE OF THE SWINDLESTOCK TAVERN 1250–1709.

1. **St Scholastica's Day plaque, Abbey House**

2. Butter Bench, Carfax, mid 18th century view

ground-floor premises for Metro Bank and student rooms above.

Walking into Queen Street, you have little sense of its ancient origins as the route to the original Westgate in the town's Saxon ramparts, but archaeological excavations have revealed traces of late Saxon occupation and road surfaces far below the present street. Queen Street was known as Great Bailey in medieval times because of its proximity to the bailey of the Norman castle founded in 1071. The City built a shambles for butchers in the centre of the street in 1556, hence the street-name Butcher Row which was used until after meat sales were transferred to the Covered Market in 1773. The 'more courtly appellation' Queen Street was adopted after a royal visit by George III and Queen Charlotte in 1785.

Most ancient houses in the street, and the butchers' shambles, were destroyed by a fire on October 6th, 1644 which began in George Street, and spread southwards into St Ebbe's, affecting between 200 and 300 houses. The shambles was rebuilt in 1655–6, and new gabled, timber-framed houses were erected on both sides of the street during the 1650s. Larger commercial buildings began to replace them later in the 19th century as Queen Street became a busy shopping street catering primarily for cash customers from Oxford's growing suburbs and nearby towns and villages. Well-known local businesses formerly included Badcock's, drapers at nos. 13–15, Kingerlee's, builders' merchants at no. 35 and, later, the Oxford & Swindon Co-operative Society Ltd. at nos. 13–17. National chain stores such as Lipton's, grocers at the late Victorian no. 44

(now Nationwide), Boots, Halford's and Home & Colonial were quick to secure premises in Queen Street, and multiples now dominate the scene. The Marks & Spencer store (1975–8, Lewis and Hickey) occupied the old Co-op site after a deal which saw the society move to the former M&S Cornmarket store. The long façade was divided into brick and rendered sections to add visual interest, and one of the company's historic clocks (c.1900) was later installed above the shop front.

Queen Street was part of the A40 until the Northern Bypass opened in 1935, and it continued to be a key route for motor traffic until the new Thames Street link was completed in 1968. Queen Street became the first major road in the city centre to be pedestrianized in 1970 and, despite its continued use by buses, the street was paved in 1973 to provide an attractive walkway to the new Westgate Centre. In an echo of the 1930s Cornmarket Street rubber road fiasco, the paving stones were soon reduced to rubble and a tarmac surface was substituted in 1975. Arguments about the sharing of road space between buses and pedestrians, and the need for a cross-town route for cyclists, continue to this day, but gazing around at Queen Street's buildings is certainly much safer than it used to be.

Walking west, you pass the glazed entrance to the Clarendon Centre (1984), which provided a welcome new arcade leading to the former Woolworths building in Cornmarket. Further along, Paperchase and Hanks Bar now occupy nos. 36–37 (1912), a gabled, half-timbered structure which, remarkably, originated as a showroom for Morris Garages. You could drive across the pavement into the ground floor of the building, and a goods lift enabled new cars to be displayed on the first floor. Morris Garages occupied these premises until their new building opened in St Aldate's in 1932. Next door, at nos. 33–35 (1888), SpecSavers and Holland and Barrett share a lofty building of red brick with stone dressings which was formerly the Wilberforce Temperance Hotel. Note the arms of the University and City beside the original main entrance, revealed when the premises were reconstructed in the 1990s.

Vision Express occupies the tall stone-fronted building, nos. 31–32 (1877), which was built as a warehouse for Hyde & Co., a wholesale clothing firm which was a major employer of local women and girls. Many were home workers, but some worked in extensive factory premises to the rear which partially survive in Shoe Lane. The Queen Street façade of Hyde's building has been shorn of some of its architectural detail, but its gargantuan scale is still evident, particularly beside the diminutive no. 30 (Costa). Curry's erected this glass-fronted building for their electrical and cycle business in 1966, replacing the last of Queen Street's 17th century timber-framed houses though

3. 36–37 Queen Street

surprisingly choosing not to go any higher. As a result, you can still see high up on the wall next door an old painted advertisement for Frank East, a draper at no. 29 from c.1880 to 1896, who then flourished in Cornmarket Street until c.1911 at premises now occupied by HSBC. This advert has reappeared in recent decades as the over-painted words 'A'Bear's Boots' have faded; A'Bear's boot and shoe shop was in nearby Castle Street.

Back on the south side, it's worth recalling the lost Electra Cinema (1911–58), the auditorium ceiling of which remained a prominent feature of the Co-op store until 1975. Beside M&S, you can see the retained stone façade of offices built for Hall's Oxford Brewery Ltd. (1914–15, Wilkins & Jeeves), which had taken over Hanley's City Brewery to the rear in 1897. Oxford City Council purchased this building to provide extra office accommodation in 1928, and called it City Chambers. Several neighbouring properties dating back to the 17th century were demolished in 1960 for a modern extension to City Chambers on the corner of St Ebbe's Street (1961, City

4. 17th century building, corner of St Ebbe's Street (demolished)

Architect's Office), which incorporated seven ground floor shops. New City Council offices and a BHS store, now a branch of the Halifax (1996, Leach Rhodes Walker) replaced this structure after less than four decades.

Reaching St Ebbe's Street today, you have a view across the paved Bonn Square towards the Tirah Memorial and New Road Baptist Church. This open space was the site of St Peter le Bailey Church, a medieval building first recorded in 1122, and then its 18th century replacement (1728–40), a rectangular stone building with a south-west tower. In 1873 the church was demolished to widen the approach to New Road, and a new church (1874, Basil Champneys) was erected in New Inn Hall Street. The former churchyard was opened up as a miniature park in 1897, and the Tirah Memorial was installed there in 1900

to commemorate officers and men of the Oxfordshire Light Infantry who died in a campaign in North-West India. The area was named Bonn Square in 1974 to honour Oxford's twin city in Germany, a link formed soon after the Second World War in 1947. Misuse of the space gave Bonn Square a poor reputation from which it never really recovered, and the area was expensively re-configured, leaving the Tirah Memorial as a centrepiece, in 2008.

Older Oxonians will recall G.R. Cooper's, the builder's merchants and ironmongers on the corner of St Ebbe's Street, and perhaps the road sign directing traffic down New Road to 'The Stations' 20 years after the LMS station had closed in 1951. The building of the Westgate Centre (1968–73, City Architect's Office) spelled the end for these features, and diverted Castle Street from its historic course. At the same time, the clearance of 19th century St Ebbe's was nearing completion, robbing St Ebbe's Street of the many local residents who had been its commercial lifeblood. The unlovely frontage of the Westgate Centre has now disappeared in its turn, masked by a continuous stone façade between St Ebbe's Street and Castle Street, which culminates in a tower and a glass lantern on the corner of the refurbished Oxfordshire County Library (2015–17, Dixon Jones).

Turning into St Ebbe's Street today, it is hard to envisage the street of small, timber-framed and gabled houses which existed here until the later 19th century; a few even survived until 1960. Like Queen Street, this was one of the original streets in the Saxon burh, leading to the ramparts on the south side where Littlegate would later be sited. By 1261–2, the street was known as Little Bailey, and it was also sometimes referred to as St Peter's Street after the church at the north end. The 1644 fire destroyed many properties in the street, but Loggan's 1675 map shows buildings on both sides of the road, apart from a short section outside Pembroke College wall. Housing development in St Ebbe's from 1820 increased the parish population from 951 in 1811 to a peak of 5,297 in 1881, and St Ebbe's Street was ideally placed to become a neighbourhood shopping centre. By 1846, it already contained 38 business premises, many of them selling food or clothing. George Randle

Cooper, a Lancastrian by origin, opened an ironmonger's shop at nos. 35–36 St Ebbe's Street, near the top of the road, in c.1879. He called his shop the City Dustpan, and promoted it by hanging a giant dustpan above the shop front. Within a few years, he could afford a house on Boar's Hill, and the retail business he founded continued to flourish until the 1970s. The Cooper site was then redeveloped for a Selfridges store (1972, T. P. Bennett & Son).

Walking down St Ebbe's Street, you pass on your right nos. 33–36 (1900, A. J. Rowley), an attractive block of shops built of red brick in the then fashionable Queen Anne style. Beyond former City Council offices, now marketed as No. 10 St Ebbe's Street, you are tempted through an archway to visit Modern Art Oxford, founded in 1966 in the surviving buildings of Hanley's City Brewery. Daniel Hanley founded this brewery in the early 19th century.

In 1877, Somerset-born Faithful Cape opened a draper's shop at no. 26 St Ebbe's Street, just below the church in an area then known as Cheapside. Cape expanded into premises above the church in the 1880s and, by 1900, the firm had a large store on the corner of St Ebbe's Street and what was then Church Street. Specialist departments took over other properties in the street, and Cape's opened branches elsewhere in Oxford. The firm was a much-loved Oxford institution with a reputation for stocking,

5. Donkey advertising Cape's store (not shown on map)

or being able to obtain, almost anything until it finally closed in 1972. Customers especially recalled the overhead cash railway which whizzed your money in a container to the central cash desk, and returned your change moments later. Initially, the four storey building (1972, T. P. Bennett & Son) on the site of Cape's housed Fenwick's glamorous fashions.

Diagonally opposite Cape's, the St Ebbe's Cash Drapery Stores opened as a business rival in c.1895, also aiming 'to supply the best qualities of goods at the lowest price for cash', not credit. The letters SPQR above the shop door harked back to the Roman slogan 'Senatus Populusque Romanus' (The Roman Senate and People), implying that all classes were welcome, but they also stood for 'Small Profits Quick Returns'. Local wits altered this to 'Simple People Quickly Robbed.' Starling's, a long-established local business specializing in carpets and lino, occupied the premises from 1967 until the present Macmillan Building for Pembroke College (1976, Sir Leslie Martin/Colin Lumley) was built on the site. The massively jettied concrete-framed structure provided more accommodation on the upper floors, and to some extent maintained the sense of the street as a narrow defile opposite St Ebbe's Church. The carved eagle at ground-floor level is a reminder that the shop premises were a branch of Barclays Bank from c.1978 to 1991.

On the other corner of Pembroke Street, the exuberant red brick, half-timbered, tile-hung and gabled Royal Blenheim pub (1898, Herbert Quinton) recalls the Victorian heyday of St Ebbe's Street. The Horse and Chair pub had been on this site since the mid 18th century, while the original Royal Blenheim, named after one of Oxford's famous stage coaches, flourished across the road

6. Cartouche, Royal Blenheim pub

on what became Cape's corner. The redevelopment of both sites provided an opportunity to rationalize things, pleasing the temperance lobby by reducing the number of pubs while providing a more appealing pub with a nostalgic name that would attract greater custom and higher profits.

From the Royal Blenheim, you get a good view of St Ebbe's church. The dedication, recorded in c.1005, is to a little-known 7th century Northumbrian saint, St Ebba, and it has been suggested that the church was a very early foundation, perhaps pre-dating the Saxon burh and associated rather with St Frideswide's monastery. Excavations to the south of the church in the 1980s tantalizingly revealed sherds of early to mid-Saxon ceramics, but the earliest burials are thought to date from the 12th century. The medieval and later church stood slightly to the south of the present site, beyond a rectory-house which was finally demolished in 1790. In 1813, William Fisher, a local builder,

7. West door, St Ebbe's Church

and a slater, William Haynes, advised the parish that the church was 'in a state of great dilapidation and danger', and recommended demolition and rebuilding. Fisher subsequently built a new St Ebbe's Church (1814–16) in Early English style on the corner of St Ebbe's Street and Church Street. The north wall of that building survives, but the new church was soon found to be too small, and what you see today dates mainly from 1862–8 when G. E. Street added a south aisle and new east windows. To accommodate the growing congregation, a west gallery was added and a new north-east door inserted (2017, Quinlan Terry). You can see the south aisle through the churchyard gate below the church. Only a handful of gravestones remain in the churchyard, but there is a wall tablet commemorating James Grainge, Mayor of Oxford, on the east wall of the south aisle. Grainge ran a jewellery and pawn-broking business in St Ebbe's which long outlived him.

By going into Pennyfarthing Place, you can see the west end of St Ebbe's Church where the tower was heightened, and bell-openings inserted in 1904–5 (A. Mardon Mowbray). Notice also the Norman doorway with its restored beak heads (c.1170) which were salvaged from the medieval church in 1813, and inserted here at the same time. Pennyfarthing Place is the surviving stub of the former Church Street which, from Saxon times until 1967, led west from here to Paradise Street and the site of the West Gate. The present street-name recalls the fact that Pembroke Street used to be known as Pennyfarthing Street, probably after William Pennyfarthing, a town bailiff in 1238. Inevitably perhaps, given Oxford's cycling pedigree, the former pub here (1973, North, Hyde & Gibbons) took the penny farthing bicycle as the inspiration for its name and the building is now the Pennyfarthing Centre, part of St Ebbe's Church. A large tree of heaven planted in the 1970s raises the spirits in this rather bleak urban setting.

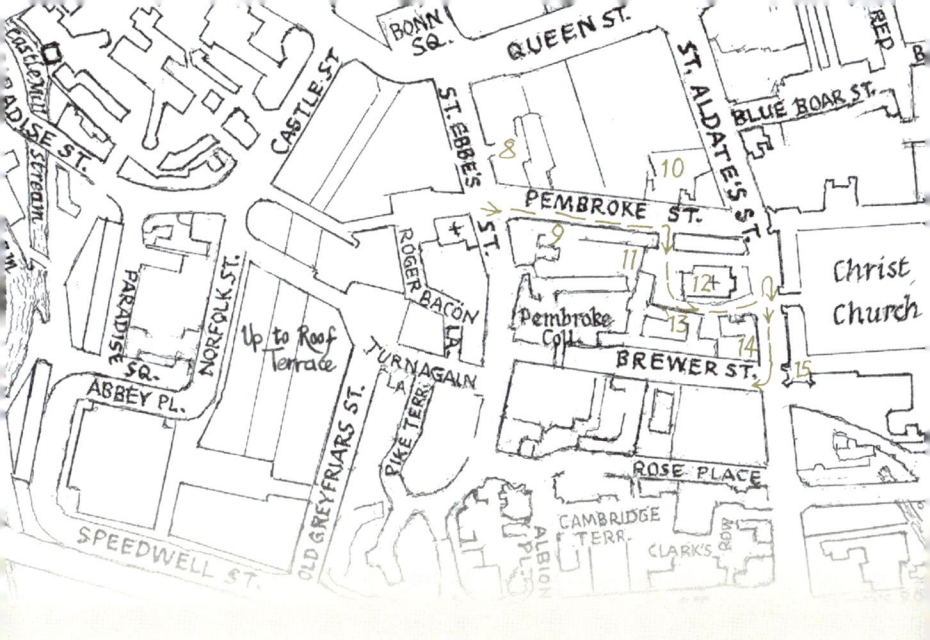

2 Pembroke Street to Christ Church

Returning to St Ebbe's Street, don't miss the wholly Victorian view over the gables of the Royal Blenheim pub towards the tower of the former City Brewery (1882, Arthur Kinder). Cross the road into Pembroke Street, one of the best preserved 'town' streets in Oxford, which retains a variety of 16th century and later houses. Many of the older properties were updated and re-fronted in the 18th and 19th centuries, and surviving shop fronts here and there recall that the street was partly commercial until modern times. The City planned to widen Pembroke Street on the south side in the early 20th century, but fortunately this scheme never progressed beyond a few properties at each end of the street, and one-way traffic was introduced in the 1930s. Pembroke College effectively saved the rest, or at least preserved their townscape value, by converting them into student accommodation. The first house beyond the Barclays Bank eagle [formerly no. 28] was retained in 1974, and the next three buildings [nos. 25–27], dating from the late 18th or early 19th centuries, were rebuilt in facsimile when other houses in this group were adapted (1966–7, C. P. Cleverly). F. Kempster, a rag and bone man, occupied no. 27 in the early 1900s, advertising his de-cluttering services with a poem which included the lines: 'Over your dwellings cast a glance, You will never have a better chance'.

On the north side, beyond the Royal Blenheim, Modern Art Oxford makes good use of the former City Brewery

8. View over gables of Royal Blenheim pub to tower of former City Brewery

stores (1888, H.G.W. Drinkwater), but the brick façade has regrettably been painted. Next door, the cavernous goods and rear entrances to M&S are tucked in beneath a plain, yellow-brick façade. They occupy the site of A. R. Mowbray & Company's printing works and church furniture workshops (1914, A. Mardon Mowbray with later additions), but much of the store is hidden behind Pembroke House, nos. 36–37, which is a five-bay, 18th century building of timber-framed construction with ruled rendering to give the appearance of stone. Each half of the property had a decorative hood over the doorway until the 1970s, but these were removed because of damage by passing traffic. The building was modified in the 19th century, with no. 36 forming part of a complex of baths, racquet courts and billiard rooms, and no. 37 housing the South Oxford Working Men's Club. Furniture removers, James Archer & Co., later known as Archer, Cowley & Co., occupied the premises from 1876, and probably formed the central archway to give access to its repository. In the 1930s, the City's Public Health Department had its offices at no. 37, and during the Second World War, staff here kept records of the thousands of children evacuated to Oxford.

Across the road, there are two timber-framed houses with jetties [nos. 23–24], the left hand one retaining a 17th century, six light oriel window on the second floor and a fine early 19th century shop front. The next house [no. 22], built in c.1800, is again timber-framed with a contemporary shop front and first floor bow window. The three storeyed diaper brick house next door [no. 21] is of c.1840 with retained ground floor shutters, whilst its neighbour [no. 20] is an early 19th century re-fronting of a 17th century timber-framed house. The arms of Queen Victoria above the cornice were probably taken from a shop with the Royal Warrant.

Back on the north side, nos. 38–39 are rather special 17th century gabled and jettied houses three storeys high. The

9. Royal arms of Queen Victoria, 20 Pembroke Street

'show' fronts are timber-framed, but the backs are simply of rubble. The original windows have all been replaced, but the remains of two oriel windows are visible beneath the gable of no. 38 and the tops of two 18th century sashes beneath the cornice of no. 39. Next door is the very tall and gabled St Aldate's Rectory (1878, J.T. Christopher) which was built of cream brick with stone quoins. It replaced an older, dilapidated building, and enabled Canon Christopher (Rector, 1859–1905) to live in the heart of the parish. Canon Cox of Cheltenham compared this building to 'a house described by Charles Dickens, which had somehow got into a crowd of smaller buildings and was quite too big ever to get out again'.

Beyond the Rectory, you reach the site of the medieval Bull Hall, one of several former academic halls in the street. Abel Parne, a baker, occupied the house during the Civil War when Brian Twyne (1580–1644), Keeper of the University Archives, and an indefatigable local antiquary, was one of his tenants. Shortly after Twyne's death, the house was destroyed in the fire of October 6th, 1644. The replacement building gave way to Rochester House and the adjacent two storey building which was formerly the Ledenporch Hall public house (1899–1900, Castle, Field & Castle). After closure in c.1920, the pub was adapted to house Oxford's first automatic telephone exchange between 1926 and 1959. When the exchange opened, Oxford had over 1,600 phone subscribers who could now dial their own local calls instead of going through the operator. These properties were acquired in 2008 for the Oxford Story Museum which opened in 2014. Don't miss the museum exhibitions in the retained 1930s K6 phone box outside.

Returning to the south side, notice the stone Cotswold-type house with three

10. Lanterns, Oxford Story Museum

storey canted bays [no. 17]. This building was erected in the early 17th century, and retains some original mullioned windows on the first and second floors. The diminutive rendered facade of no. 16 is followed by a three storeyed 18th century house [no. 15] built of rendered and painted ashlar stone with a moulded stone parapet. Moses or Moyses Hall had occupied this site in medieval times, named after the original Jewish owner of the site in the 12th century. Nos. 13–14 were built as a single grand house by Richard Hannes, a local brewer, in 1641. There are two storeys of rendered rubble topped by a two storey timber-framed superstructure which was modernized in the 18th century. The fine central pedimented doorway is not original, and the subdivision of the building led to the insertion of a second door to its right. The next house [no. 12] has a plain three storey stuccoed front with a moulded stone bracketed hood over the door.

Pembroke Street ends pleasantly on the north side with nos. 43–44, early 19th century chequer-brick houses, and no. 45, which is 17th century and timber framed with one large gable facing the street. This building was fortunate to escape a fire on 29 June 1870 which destroyed adjacent properties in St Aldate's at a cost of two lives, and led directly to the formation of the Oxford Volunteer Fire Brigade. On the south side, beyond the alleyway to Pembroke Square, no. 11 is a three storey stuccoed house with a first floor overhang and a second floor string course; unusually, the ground floor is weather-boarded. Old properties beyond here were demolished, and the building line set back for the tall brick range (1913) which extends towards the corner of St Aldate's.

Return to the alleyway between nos. 11 and 12 Pembroke Street and walk into Pembroke Square, adjusting to the unaccustomed light on a sunny day.

11. View through iron gates of Beef Lane and Besse Building, Pembroke College

Behind you, notice the handsome south elevation of nos. 13–14 Pembroke Street which has a projecting staircase tower flanked by a gabled bay on each side. Jetties at second floor and attic storey level have enriched pendants. Further along, there are glimpses of the backs of the other Pembroke Street houses that now form staircases in Pembroke College North Quad. The street-name plate Beef Lane high up on the College wall in front of you is a reminder of the ancient street which cut through from here to St Ebbe's Street. Its name was derived from Beef Hall, a 14th century academic hall named after the Bella Fago family. Old stone houses on the south side of the lane were demolished for Pembroke's Chapel Quad in the 1840s, and the formation of North Quad led in 1961 to the clearance of remaining houses on the north side, some dating back to the early 17th century. Beef Lane, then described as a 'little-used street', was closed as a public thoroughfare in 1960, but you can peer through the iron gates towards Pembroke's Besse Building (1956, Worthington & Sons), a three storey ashlar stone building with canted bay windows, very old-fashioned for the time. The Macmillan Building (1976, Sir Leslie Martin/Colin Lumley), which we saw from St Ebbe's Street, rears up behind it.

Turning back, you have a fine view of St Aldate's Church and especially the tower and slender spire (1873–4, J. T. Christopher) which play a strong supporting role in distant views of Oxford's dreaming spires. St Aldate's Church is first recorded in the early 12th century, but its name, presumably a corruption of 'old gate', suggests a much older foundation. Recent excavations in

12. Figurative panels on 1961 extension to Aldate's Church

the church have confirmed that burials were taking place on the site in the 9th and 10th centuries. Burials continued in the small churchyard surrounding the church until the mid19th century, and you can still find a few gravestones among the bikes in the paved area north of the tower. The early burial registers for St Aldate's have been lost, so memorials such as those to Mary, wife of Richard Colton (d.1678) and William Pierson (d. 1667) are more than usually significant. Now heading past the west end of the church towards Pembroke College, notice the single storey stone extension (1961) which provided additional facilities for the church. Small decorative panels illustrate features in the parish such as Alice's Shop, Morris Garages, and the Central Library, then still in the Town Hall. Note also the sculpture above the south doorway of this building which shows Jesus preaching to a 20th century crowd.

Pembroke College was founded on the site of the medieval Broadgates Hall in 1624. Nominally, the founder was James I, but the money came from a successful Oxfordshire maltster, Thomas Tesdale, and Richard Wightwick, a Shropshire clergyman. The College was named after the Earl of Pembroke, then Chancellor of the University. The gate-tower and the north range of Old Quad date from 1673–94, and the range to the right of the College entrance was built as the Master's Lodgings by 1695. These buildings were originally classical in style, but they were elaborately Gothicized by Daniel Evans, a local builder, in 1829–30, and Bodley & Garner added a parapet to the gate-tower in 1879.

From the College entrance, you have a splendid view across Pembroke Square with its mix of cobbles and stone setts towards St Aldate's Church. Tom Tower in Christ Church is beautifully framed by the mature lime tree at the corner of the churchyard. St Aldate's Church was considerably altered during the 19th century, and not least on this side by

13. Oriel window, Pembroke College

the partial demolition (1838–43) of the chantry chapel built in c.1334 by John of Ducklington (d. c.1336), a fishmonger and Mayor of Oxford eleven times. Broadgates Hall was using an upper room as a library by 1544, and the building served as Pembroke College library and chapel until the 18th century. H. J. Underwood was the architect responsible for the drastic re-shaping of the south aisle, which retains 14th century decorated windows, but the church was then considerably altered and extended while Canon Christopher was rector (1862 and 1873–4, J.T. Christopher). Notice on the south wall of the church the re-sited reredos commemorating the parishioners killed in the Great War.

Today's comparatively wide entrance to Pembroke Square from St Aldate's dates back to the mid 1830s. Prior to that, Pembroke College was approached by little more than a passageway. To the north, there was a row of timber-framed houses, probably dating back to the late 16th century between the east end of the church and the street.

To the south stood the north range of the Christ Church almshouses, begun by Cardinal Wolsey in c.1525 as part of his Cardinal College project, and re-founded by Christ Church in 1546. In 1834, following complex negotiations, Christ Church agreed to remove their part of the obstruction, and 'lay open the new front of Pembroke College' provided that the Paving Commissioners, the highway authority, acquired and demolished the offending houses.

Turn left into St Aldate's to visit the church although it is rarely open outside published service times. Canon Christopher made St Aldate's the centre of evangelical influence in the City and University, and that tradition is very much alive today. The church interior was much altered in the 19th century, and recently reordered (1999, Batterton Tyack Architects), but the chancel building retains traces of Norman arcading. The north aisle originated in c.1456 as a chantry chapel established by Philip Polton (d.1461), Archdeacon of Gloucester and Fellow of All Souls. The very much restored south aisle (c.1334) was John of Ducklington's chantry chapel. The altar-tomb of John Noble (d.1522), Principal of Broadgates Hall, stands in the chancel; nearby, you can see the fragment of a 10th century carved cross shaft excavated in 1999.

Outside the church, you can appreciate the sheer scale of the St Aldate's front of Christ Church. Thomas Wolsey secured papal permission to suppress St Frideswide's Priory in 1524, and he also acquired further land and premises for his ambitious new foundation, Cardinal College. The topography of the area was transformed, streets were closed and houses demolished. Lost streets included Jury or Civil School Lane, running east from St Aldate's just north of Pembroke Street, and Frideswide Lane, opposite St Aldate's Church.

The building of Cardinal College began in 1525 but the St Aldate's frontage had only progressed a little way north of the gate-house when Wolsey fell from royal favour and died in 1529. By then, the gate-house had been finished to roof level, and the footings of the vast chapel which Wolsey envisaged for the north side of the quad had been completed. Henry VIII soon took over Wolsey's foundation and he re-founded it as Christ Church in 1546, but the St Aldate's front was only completed as a mirror image of the south range in 1668. This symmetry was not originally intended, for an archaeological excavation in the 1960s revealed footings of the west wall of Wolsey's chapel outside the north range. Tom Tower (1681–2, Christopher Wren) finally completed and perfected the 16th century gate-house after the architect advised Dean Fell that he had 'resolved it ought to be Gothic to agree with the Founder's work.'

Cross Pembroke Square opposite Tom Tower and walk down St Aldate's

14. Christ Church almshouses, from a sketch c.1830

towards Brewer Street. The ground falls away quite considerably at this point, and this part of the street was sometimes known as Tower Hill. The two storey Christ Church front has a basement at its southern end, and you will notice that the lower doorway to the former Christ Church almshouses is some four feet above the pavement, presumably because of changes to footway levels. The almshouses initially accommodated 24 almsmen, each of whom received a yearly pension of six pounds. Draft statutes in 1546 required inmates to 'make no outragiouse noyse in your Alms howse', to 'goe only to honest places and for honest purposes', and 'at all tymes indeavour youre selves to be well occupied and at no tyme to be ydell (sic).' The almshouses were restored (1834, H. J. Underwood) when the north range was demolished, but the last inmates, Crimean War veterans, were removed in 1868. Christ Church sold the buildings to Pembroke College in 1888, and they became the Master's Lodgings in 1928.

The Christ Church front ends with a projecting bay which has two polygonal projections decorated with Cardinals' hats. The coving of the large oriel window between them playfully combines Wolsey's shield, emblems and motto with putti, or little naked boys. This panel is the earliest example of the Renaissance style in Oxford, and the only one in the original work at Christ Church. The medieval church of St Michael at the South Gate (c.1122–1525) stood on this site, and was another casualty of Wolsey's scheme. The church may have formed part of the defences like St Michael at the North Gate church in Cornmarket. The South Gate was described as 'an ornament to that end of the towne, well guarded on each side with a

15. Carved stone putti, Christ Church

large fortification, and adorned with battlements on the top and ... the armes of England and France quartered'. Part of the gate was presumably demolished for Cardinal College, and the rest fell down in 1617.

3 Brewer Street to Clark's Row

Brewer Street lay just outside the South Gate, and originated as a lane between the Saxon ramparts and the Trill Mill Stream, a branch of the River Thames now lost beneath Rose Place. Turning into the street, you are immediately aware of the old city wall as the dominant feature on your right. In 1630, the City permitted Pembroke College to build upon the wall, charging 1s 8d (8p) a year for the privilege. Although the wall is much patched and indeed replaced by ashlar stone beneath the College chapel, it has survived substantially intact, unlike the section beyond Littlegate.

In medieval times, Brewer Street led to the great friaries in St Ebbe's, but the proximity of water, for brewing, for power, and for refuse disposal encouraged industrial development. The street is so called because brewing took place here, perhaps from as early as the 13th century until 1933. In 1310, Edward II ruled that butchers should no longer slaughter animals at Carfax or other public places, and many moved here to what was sometimes known as Slaying Lane between c.1478 and 1819. Trill Mill Stream provided the ideal receptacle for animal remains, and in c.1500 members of the Leke family, local brewers, were charged with throwing dung and 'loggell' into the stream.

The street hardly seems to have been a place for high-quality housing, but long narrow properties on the south side meant that well-off brewers, in particular,

16. Campion Hall with part of Christ Church Cathedral School on left, Brewer Street

were able to live there very comfortably with much of their business out of sight and smell. No. 1 Brewer Street, the first property on the left, is a substantial ashlar stone house dating from 1596, although it has since undergone many modifications with some windows gone and others blocked. No. 2 was built in c.1620 by Oliver Smith, brewer and Mayor of Oxford in 1629, who called it Slaughter House, presumably as a jest. During the Civil War, both properties were occupied by Thomas Smith, another member of the local brewing dynasty, and the Earl of Forth, Lord Lieutenant of the Royalist Army, was among his lodgers. Note the plaque to the author and scholar Dorothy Sayers (1893–1957) beside the door of no. 1, recalling that she was born here. No. 2 was later divided into three properties, and only the ground floor stone work and some fine interior details survived rebuilding (1933, Coleridge, Jennings & Soimenow). Continuing west, no. 3, Christ Church Cathedral School (1892, H. W. Moore) is of red brick with stone dressing, and brings a breath of North Oxford into the city centre. Almost opposite, a low cast iron bollard supplied by the former Temple Street foundry, Dean & Son, protects the base of the city wall from damage.

Beyond the school, Campion Hall (1936, Sir Edwin Lutyens) makes interesting use of a relatively confined site, presenting towards St. Aldate's 'the polygonal east end of the chapel elevated above a ground floor with two round arches.' The building provided a permanent home for an institution that had been founded by the Jesuits as a private college for Catholics in 1895. The far end of Lutyens' façade incorporates the rubble stone remains of Micklem Hall, to which he added a Roman Doric doorcase of c.1740 brought from elsewhere. Micklem Hall had latterly been a private academic hall but in 1644, it was home to Edward Carpenter, a graduate of St John's College who, unusually, was both a barrister and a brewer. An old malthouse attached to this brewery still backed on to Rose Place in 1935.

Opposite Campion Hall, notice the blocked arches of two drain exits low down in the city wall. The south range of Pembroke College Old Quad (1626) rises impressively above the wall and retains original dormer windows to the attics. The ashlar stone College chapel (1732) led to the rebuilding of a portion of the city wall, but the old wall resumes below the Fellows' Garden. Ancient stone bollards protect the wall from damage, and luxuriant overhanging shrubs make this a picturesque sight in all seasons. Since 2012, a glass-sided bridge, soon dubbed 'the Bridge of Thighs', has crossed Brewer Street at this point, providing an elegant link with a new Pembroke College development (2013, Berman Guedes Stretton) which extends west to Littlegate Street and south to Rose Place. On the south side of Brewer Street, the development took in a site occupied since c.1949 by Hall the Printer Ltd., and in the late 19th century by stables for Oxford's tram horses. It also incorporated two listed buildings, nos. 7 and 8 Brewer Street. Both have stuccoed stone ground floors and rendered timber-framing on the upper floors. No. 7 is a late 18th century re-fronting of a 17th century house with fashionable bow windows set back within the frontage. This was a feature required by Oxford's Paving Commissioners after 1771 to avoid obstructing the pavement. A wall-plaque on no. 8 records that these properties were named Bannister Building after Sir Roger Bannister (Master of Pembroke College 1985-93).

At the end of Brewer Street, notice opposite a wall-plaque which recalls Littlegate, first mentioned in 1244. This gate in the city wall consisted of a small arched gateway for pedestrians and a larger one for carts. Scholars were renting a room over Littlegate in 1323–4, and again in 1414–15, despite the University's growing disapproval of unsupervised students. The cart gateway was falling down in the early 17th century, but the pedestrian arch survived until 1798. Littlegate was sometimes called Water Gate because it was near a ford at Trill Mill Stream 'necessary for the inhabitants thereabouts to water cattle,' and Milk Street as an alternative name for Littlegate Street presumably derived from cattle grazing on the riverside meadows.

The Pure Gym building above the Littlegate wall-plaque (1972, Collins Stonebridge & Bradley) replaced a row of Victorian shops which served the large local population; passages through those properties once led to crowded yards at the back. Looking up St Ebbe's

17. Littlegate from a sketch by John Malchair

Street from the corner of Brewer Street, Pembroke College Hall (1848, John Hayward) rises impressively above the blackened stone boundary wall. The space beneath the wall now features a monumental stone-clad sub-station, and provides a few parking places. Until the 1930s, several gabled, timber-framed 17th century houses occupied the area nearest Beef Lane. Baboo Mookhi Singh, Oxford's first Asian shopkeeper, ran a grocer's shop at one of these properties in the 1890s.

Turn left into Littlegate Street, where your view in medieval times would have been dominated by the great friaries; from the mid16th century until the early 19th century you would have been heading past a few houses towards riverside meadows and, later, market gardens. Then, within two decades, streets and houses took over this low-lying area and, until the 1960s, you would at this point have been walking towards the populous suburb of St Ebbe's, also known as The Friars. Given Oxford's reputation as an unchanging city, extraordinarily little of this history survives today, but archaeological excavations, documentary research and people's memories help to re-create the lost townscapes which we'll explore later in the walk.

Across Littlegate Street, the 17th century rubble stone wall south of Littlegate House is on the site of the 13th century

18. Victorian Drinking Fountain, now removed

precinct wall which marked the eastern boundary of the Greyfriars. Part of the wall was demolished for a garage entrance in the 1960s, dislodging a Victorian drinking fountain (1859) donated by Oxford M.P., James Haughton Langston, to provide pure water in an area of polluted wells. On the east side of Littlegate Street, the Pembroke College development (2013, Berman Guedes Stretton) and Albion House (1973) replaced old properties, the last of which went in 1961. An earlier casualty was the decrepit building where students from Balliol College established Balliol Boys' Club in 1906. The street today can seem almost eerily quiet, but it buzzed with life then as dozens of St Ebbe's boys came along to play games and enjoy supervised activities. In 1921, the club was re-housed to new premises in Blackfriars Road. It was named Keith Rae House after a former Balliol undergraduate who had been killed in the Great War and continued to flourish until St Ebbe's was cleared. Tony Del Nevo, an Italian immigrant, opened a fried fish shop at no. 7 Littlegate Street in 1894 which his family continued to run until 1969. The wholesale confectioners, Oxford Candy Stores, had premises on the site of Albion House for many decades.

Beyond the Littlegate House garage entrance, you would formerly have reached Trill Mill Stream, now an almost forgotten branch of the River Thames which disappears into a culvert behind Paradise Square, and is piped through the Westgate development and beneath Littlegate Street before re-emerging in Christ Church Memorial Garden. The course of the River Thames through Oxford has long been subject to change,

19. Trill Mill Stream in Littlegate Street, from a sketch by B. C. Buckler, c.1820

and today's attenuated stream is all that is left of a major channel that once flowed through St Ebbe's and across the northern edge of Christ Church Meadow to join the Cherwell. By the 11th century, two streams had been dug running south from this channel, one west of St Aldate's serving a mill later known as Blackfriars Mill, and another east of St Aldate's serving Trill Mill. Providing water to these mills, and a possible Greyfriars mill, became the main purpose of a canalized Trill Mill Stream, and its name is thought to derive from the sound of water rushing through them. The river channel continuing across Christ Church Meadow gradually silted up before being entirely lost in the 17th century.

The Blackfriars built a bridge over Trill Mill Stream at this point before 1285, and it was later known as Preachers' Bridge. The various mills reliant on Trill Mill Stream probably ceased to work by the mid 16th century but, as we have seen in Brewer Street, brewers and maltsters continued to make use of the waterway. Tanners too had been recorded in St Ebbe's by 1279, and the tanning of leather probably took place beside Trill Mill Stream for centuries. Littlegate Tanyard occupied a large site beyond Preachers' Bridge on the west side of Littlegate Street. In the early 19th century, Alderman Thomas Bricknell owned the site, and built a large stone house beside tan pits that were said to take over 2,000 hides. Mortgage debts forced Bricknell to sell up in 1823, but the tanyard continued as a going concern until it was destroyed by fire in c.1865. Houses quickly occupied the site in the late 1860s, long after the rest of St Ebbe's had been developed.

Littlegate Tanyard was a major source of pollution, but when Henry Taunt, the

Oxford photographer, was growing up in St Ebbe's in the 1840s, local people were still fetching water from Trill Mill Stream for washing purposes. Taunt's childhood revolved around the stream, fishing in it, boating along its length and sometimes falling in. By this time, however, the waterway was fast becoming an open sewer, and Taunt recalled that 'every dwelling had its house of easement built out over the stream, and filth of every kind was simply tossed into its course.' Trill Mill Stream acquired the ironic nickname Pactolus from a legendary stream in Lydia which had sands of pure gold. In the 1860s, Oxford's Paving Commissioners, unable to solve the City's wider drainage problems, chose the easier option of burying Trill Mill Stream between Paradise Square and Christ Church Meadow. By 1880, a new main drainage system had cleaned up the Thames in Oxford, but too late to save Trill Mill Stream as the valued feature in the townscape it might have become.

Albion Place was so-called by 1850 when the street name applied only to the small area between Trill Mill Stream and now vanished houses beside what is now the Oxford Centre for the Deaf and Hard of Hearing. We shall explore that remarkable building shortly in the context of the Blackfriars and the later history of St Ebbe's, so turn left past Staincross House (1973) and into Rose Place, a lane created (1862–4) above the course of the culverted Trill Mill Stream. On your left, the south front of the Pembroke College development (2013, Berman Guedes Stretton) was a welcome addition to the local scene. Across the road, new traffic-friendly street layouts in the 1960s spawned buildings with rounded corners such as Southern House, originally Mowbray's bookshop (1971, Marshman Warren Taylor), and Hogreve House, built as the local headquarters of the Salvation Army (1970–1, John Fryman; alterations, 2011) to replace the Victorian red brick Salvation Army Citadel in Castle Street.

Walking along Rose Place, you pass the rear elevation of 18th century Clark's House on your right. The Blackfriars millstream ran along its eastern boundary, beginning opposite the rubble stone wall behind Christ Church Cathedral School. Archer's brewery in St Aldate's was still using this stream in the 1830s, but the silted-up ditch had been entirely covered in as a health hazard by 1876. You now come to the four storey buff brick Catholic Chaplaincy (1970-1, Ahrends Burton and Koralek). This building, a succession of stepped façades with bay windows, reveals the spectacular timber-framed side elevation of nos. 86–87 St Aldate's, the Old Palace. The house was formerly known as Bishop King's Palace after Robert King, the first Bishop of Oxford (d.1557), but the building post-dates him, and no bishop has ever lived here. The house was built in two sections, the smaller west range probably by the tanner, Edward Barkesdale (d.1596). Thomas Smith, from the ubiquitous

20. Carved brackets, Bishop King's Palace

brewing family, later acquired the property, and added the main house abutting St Aldate's (c.1622–8). The older part has two gables, and the newer portion five large gables. The elevation is jettied, and the upper floors have pargetted decoration and oriel windows. Each oriel rests on three brackets carved with grotesques and the middle one on the first floor bears the date 1628. By contrast, the east elevation is of ashlar stone with a Dutch gable. Unton Croke (c.1595–1671), a Member of Parliament and Parliamentary sympathizer, bought the main house in 1637. During the Civil War, he chose to live more discreetly at his house in Marston where the treaty for the surrender of Oxford was eventually signed in 1646. From 1655 to 1669, the building was used as a girls' boarding school, nicknamed Virgins' Hall. By the end of the 19th century, the Old Palace was in a poor condition, and the historian Herbert Hurst described tawdry additions on the north side as 'a fungoid growth on the mansion.' The building was sympathetically restored (1919, F. F. Mullett) as part of the architect's unrealized scheme to build a Franciscan priory church of St Nicholas behind it. A further restoration took place in 1952–3 when the east elevation was re-fronted.

Emerging from Rose Place before the mid1920s, you would have found yourself in one of the narrowest parts of St Aldate's opposite the three storey Green Dragon Inn (c. 1796). Road-widening then claimed this building and its neighbours, but you are compensated by exceptional views of Christ Church and Christ Church Memorial Garden (1927) before turning right into Clark's Row beyond no. 85 St Aldate's. No. 85 is a late 18th century three storey house with a stuccoed front, perhaps masking an earlier building. The first floor bay window was added in 1877, and the Georgian-style shop front is modern. Across Clark's Row, no. 84 has an 18th century four storey front of rendered timber framing with sash windows on the upper floors. As is so often the case, this plain façade masks a much older building which, in part, dates back to c.1600. Behind this frontage, Thomas Seymour, a college servant at All Souls, added a timber-framed property in 1637 which has been dismantled and the frame restored as part of a still to be realized project to create two houses on the site; documentary research shows that Seymour shared his house with Royal servants during the Civil War. Clark's Row at first retains its road surface of stone setts, but a group of 18th century rendered timber-framed houses behind no. 85 St Aldate's was demolished in the 1960s. The row today is diverted around the Catholic Chaplaincy, and you pass on your left a stretch of ancient rubble walling with a post-medieval wooden shutter. This is thought to have been built towards the end of the 16th century as the rear wall for a two storey range of service rooms behind Littlemore Hall; these rooms were later converted into five cottages known as Littlemore Court which survived until the 1930s. You are

21. Post medieval wooden shutter

now behind the bulky Speedwell House (1972–4, Olins John Associates) which occupied the Bridewell Square site at the corner of St Aldate's and Speedwell Street. The developers wished to bring the Carfax Conduit back from Nuneham Park to provide an architectural feature, but nothing came of the idea.

By working your way around the Catholic Chaplaincy building, you return to the original alignment of Clark's Row which crossed the Blackfriars mill-stream before continuing as a footpath to Cambridge Terrace. Almost miraculously, this black-bricked path between stone walls has been retained but, before you set off along it, notice the square gate-posts, which introduce Clark's House, no. 7 Clark's Row, away to your right. This house is probably mid-late 18th century in origin, being a two storey, stuccoed building with canted bays either side of a central doorway which is approached by steps; later additions to the right extended over the culverted mill-stream. Now hemmed in by other buildings, the house originally had extensive gardens and open views towards the River Thames. By the late 19th century it had become a mother and baby hostel, run at first by the Oxford City Moral Welfare Association and later by social services. It was known for many years as Skene House after Felicia Skene (1821–99), the Oxford social reformer and prison visitor who lived in St Michael's Street.

Another pair of gate-posts formerly stood to the south of the black brick path, and led into Union Place, described in 1935 as 'a row of very good uniform mid 18th century three-storeyed cottages'. Peter Cousins, the owner of one of these properties, disputed a compulsory purchase order in 1967 on the grounds that they formed an architectural group with Clark's House. The Ministry's Inspector supported the City's wish to create a spacious setting outside the

22. Littlemore Court from a photograph by Henry Minn, 1910

new Magistrates' Court, arguing that, 'if the houses were left, the backs of them would face the entrance to the court and washing might be left hanging outside.' Today's open space planted with plane trees is the outcome, and people attending Oxford Magistrates' Court (1966–9, City Architect's Office/Douglas Murray) are never distracted by the sight of intimate garments blowing in the wind!

Continue along the path into Cambridge Terrace, now a street of modern buildings, but still on the alignment established when Treadwell's market garden in the former Blackfriars precinct was laid out for building in the 1830s. The Church Army established a training house in St Aldate's in 1884, and ran a hostel for working men at premises on the north side of Cambridge Terrace from c.1894 to 1972. This building was used as a war kitchen during the First World War to provide local people with cheap, wholesome meals at a time of food shortages and rising prices. Cambridge Street, now lost beneath the Magistrates' Court and the gargantuan Telephone Exchange (1954–7, Ministry of Works), formerly ran south from Cambridge Terrace. The line of Albert Street survives in part at the end of Cambridge Terrace, but the street name Albion Place was extended south to Speedwell Street in 1980, displacing the old name which presumably derived from the Prince Consort who married Queen Victoria in 1840.

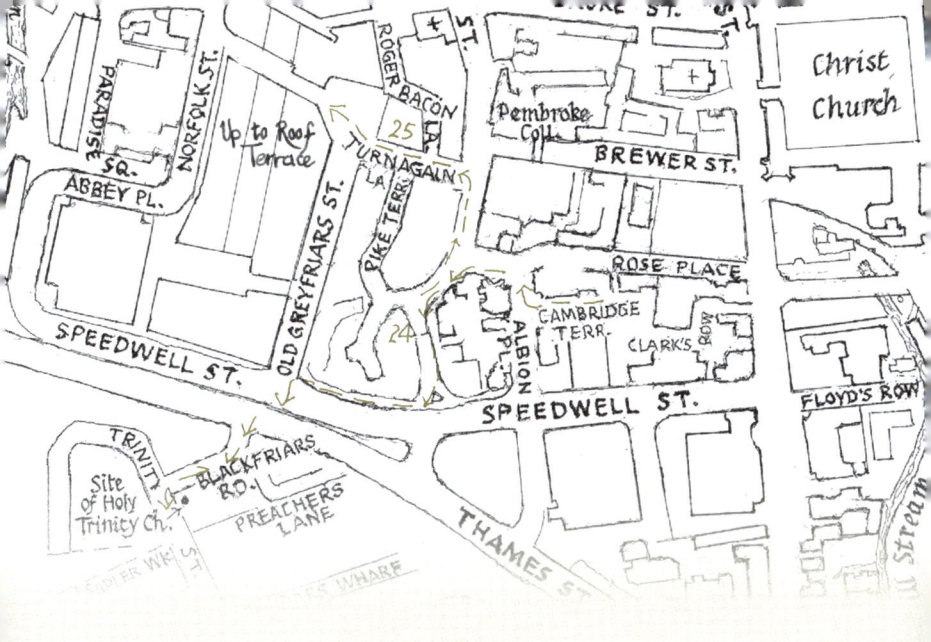

4 The Friars and St Ebbe's

Turn right into Albion Place, and make for no. 10 Littlegate Street, a building of huge historical significance and occupied since 1968 by the Oxford Centre for the Deaf and Hard of Hearing. The hornbeam tree in the car park was planted then to mark the restoration of the two storey rubble stone building. The inner doorway to the projecting porch bears the date 1647 but, during restoration, the late medieval arched gateway of the nearby Blackfriars was rediscovered in the west wall of the building, having been hidden from view for over a century. The first Dominicans, or Blackfriars, arrived in Oxford in 1221, and established a base in the heart of the Jewry. They soon found the premises too confined and, helped by generous benefactors, they 'translated themselves to a pleasant isle in the South Suburbs.'

Their new precinct, acquired in 1236, ran south from here towards the River Thames and east to the mill-stream parallel to St Aldate's. Building was soon under way, and the friars were able to move in by 1245. The church was finally consecrated in 1262, and fresh water was brought to the site by conduit from Hinksey Hill (c.1280). Excavations during the St. Ebbe's redevelopment (1961–75) confirmed that the plan of the priory was quite conventional, with a large church – probably the largest Dominican church in England – at the northern end of the site, a great cloister and chapter house to the south, and a little cloister beyond

23. A Blackfriar (not shown on map)

that. The 'pleasant isle' was of course very prone to flooding, and the friars raised the ground surface within the priory as well as building flood defences outside it. The completed priory became the *studium*, or place of study, for the English province of the Dominican Order, and ultimately one of four serving the whole Order.

For almost 300 years, the great Blackfriars buildings dominated this locality. In the early 16th century, the priory was still receiving substantial benefactions and bequests, and people were still choosing to be buried in the church. All this changed quickly when Henry VIII broke away from Rome. The house surrendered to the King's commissioners in July 1538, and its plate was soon packed off to the royal safe. In 1544, William Frere, an Oxford entrepreneur and his wife Agnes acquired the site, and rapidly demolished most of the buildings. Stone from here was used for new walls around Trinity College and in what is now Blue Boar Street. By 1578, scarcely any standing buildings were left, and Anthony Wood commented that the Blackfriars site was now 'a peice *(sic)* of ground desolate and naked'. Thomas Treadwell established a market garden in the area in the 18th century.

Behind no. 10 Littlegate Street, the stone-built former Adullam chapel (1832, William Fisher) is one of a handful of 19th century buildings in St Ebbe's to survive an extraordinarily thorough cull. The chapel was founded by the Rev Henry Bulteel (1800–66), a curate of St Ebbe's ejected from the Church of England in 1831 because of his controversial theological views. The building became a Baptist chapel until c.1938, with a Sunday School at the front and the minister's house behind. It was used as a Food Office during wartime and post-war rationing, and blood donors currently have the opportunity to experience the chapel interior at regular sessions. Behind this building, flats occupy the site of Lucy Faithfull House, built originally as a Church Army Hostel (1976–8, Oxford Architects Partnership; demolished 2018). The building was re-named to honour the work of Baroness Faithfull of Wolvercote (1910–96), social worker and children's campaigner, who was children's officer

24. Shop in Commercial Road from an old photograph (demolished)

and director of social services in Oxford from 1958 to 1974.

It is now almost as challenging to explore the 19th century Friars district as it is to conjure up the lost friaries, but the short walk to Speedwell Street provides a few clues and illustrates the tortuous process by which the area has been redeveloped. Faulkner Street, alongside the former chapel, was formerly Commercial Road, laid out in 1819 as a route to the new gasworks then being erected in a meadow by the river. When Alderman Bricknell, owner of the Littlegate Tanyard, began to sell off his land in 1820, a new road, Friars Street, was linked to the access road to the gasworks, and the first plots were made available for small houses in this low-lying area. Richard Wootten, an Oxford banker, sold off meadowland south of Friars Street in

1822, and houses were soon being built in a long parallel road, Blackfriars Road, and in Gas Street near the gasworks.

The building of St Ebbe's or The Friars was virtually complete by the late 1830s, leaving just Paradise Square, Friars Wharf and the Littlegate Tanyard undeveloped. The rush to build reflected the rapid growth of the city's population from 11,921 in 1801 to 24,258 by 1841, an increase swelled by migration from the countryside. The demolition of old properties for college buildings and other improvements also stimulated housing demand. Most St Ebbe's houses were two or three storey terraced houses of brick and slate with a patch of garden ground at the back, but some courtyard developments differed little from the congested yards behind Oxford's main streets. The quality of building was moderately high and the sanitary failings of the area were largely due to piecemeal development and the inadequate drainage and water supply.

From the 1870s, mains drainage and the supply of clean water remedied some of these defects, and the City began to improve living conditions by issuing nuisance removal orders and closing the worst courts. In 1919, the Rectors of St Ebbe's and St Aldate's were prominent signatories to a petition to the Medical Officer of Health, complaining about the unhealthiness of the area, and urging greater action. Slum clearance areas were identified in the 1930s, and a redevelopment plan for St Ebbe's went to the Minister of Health in early 1939. The outbreak of war prevented further progress on this scheme, but wholesale clearance began in the 1950s with the tacit understanding that former residents who wished to return would be able to do so when the area had been redeveloped. Unfortunately, the re-planning of St Ebbe's was complicated by uncertainties over the route of Oxford's inner relief road and political debates as to the appropriate balance between business and housing.

Over 900 properties were eventually demolished, leaving just four buildings from the 19th century suburb – a chapel, two pubs and the rectory – and wiping many streets off the map. By 1974, Alderman Fred Ingram was describing the destruction of The Friars and the scattering of the community as 'the biggest mistake Oxford ever made.' In considering how this happened, it is important to remember that most contemporary opinion, and government policy, viewed the clearance of outworn houses and the provision of spacious modern housing as the truly progressive option. A more positive attitude to historic buildings was gradually emerging, and 65 19th century houses in St Ebbe's were provisionally listed in the 1950s although all were subsequently demolished. Few local property owners chose to resist the loss of blighted properties that needed expensive modernization and generated low rents.

The residents of St Ebbe's, most of them tenants, had little say in the process, and they were in any case divided among themselves. Some loved the area, and nostalgic Friars' reunions were held annually until 1982, but others probably echoed a former resident's view that her new house in Barton 'was like heaven after what we've been used to'.

From the railings in Speedwell Street, you can see the consequences of this complicated history. Speedwell Street originated as the medieval Overee Lane, leading from St Aldate's to Blackfriars. In the 1830s, it was extended west to link up with Commercial Road when Treadwell's Garden was laid out for building. In the 1950s, Speedwell Street was envisaged as the likely link between a Christ Church Meadow road and Oxpens Road, and the City embarked on the Preachers Lane council housing scheme (1960–2, City Architects Office) of flats and maisonettes in front of you. A later phase would have reached Speedwell Street, but the decision to build a new Thames Street link road in 1967 halted the development, and you will notice that Thames Street passes uncomfortably close to the nearest block.

Faulkner Street is now choked off at Speedwell Street, but the former Commercial Road continued straight into Friars Wharf, a late 1840s cul-de-sac built over a dock rendered obsolete by the coming of the railways. A wharf house (c.1830) built on the dockside survived to become the Wharf House pub, and it was again retained in the 1960s when the rest of the area was cleared. You can see the little ashlar stone building among the trees on the rounded-off corner linking Speedwell Street and Thames Street. It was incorporated into a small council housing development (1982, City Architect's Office) and, after closing as a pub, it was converted to residential use (2007, Riach Architects).

Away to your right, beyond the traffic lights and grass banks constructed as noise barriers, you may like to explore a short surviving section of Blackfriars Road on its 1820s alignment. The road is now lined by plane trees rather than houses built on the pavement edge, and it extends only as far as Trinity Street, where Holy Trinity Church (1844–5, H. J. Underwood; demolished 1957) formerly stood. A few doors away, no. 84 Blackfriars Road (c.1830), a good three storey brick building, survived until 1978 when it was the last 19th century house in St Ebbe's to be demolished. The northward continuation of Trinity Street across Blackfriars Road, now swiftly diverted away from Thames Street, is a reminder of a late Victorian improvement. No thought had originally been given to forming a connection between Blackfriars Road and Friars Street but, in 1890, the City cleared several old properties in both roads, and extended Trinity Street across the site to form a link road and open up the area. West of this junction, large gasometers across the river dominated the houses in Blackfriars Road until 1968. Now, that section of the road is lost in the housing development (1979–83, Architects Design Partnership) which was wrapped around the earlier Preachers Lane housing. The scheme included both council and private houses, and enabled a few former residents of The Friars to return 'home'. Vi King told the *Oxford Mail*: 'I'm over the moon. It's lovely just to hear the trains go by'. The street names, Dale Close and Sadler Walk, recall two of the district's lost streets. For a brief detour, turn left into Trinity Street and right into Sadler Walk to reach Castle Mill Stream and, away to the left, the retained Gasworks Bridge (1886, Thomas Hawksley) over the main river which enabled coal to be delivered into the gasworks by rail.

Heading back to Littlegate Street, you have striking views of the John Lewis store (2015–17, Glenn Howells Architects) and the south façade of the Westgate extension (2015–17, Panter Hudspeth). These tall steel-framed structures with few windows in their panelled brick facades look almost defensive in character; a modern equivalent of the massive 13th century stone wall around the Greyfriars precinct which archaeologists revealed during excavations on the site. Westgate's Old Greyfriars Street elevation dominates a low-rise council housing development (1987, City Architect's Office) which occupied a site proposed for a relocated Covered Market or Crown Courts under earlier unrealized plans. These houses represented an attempt by the City to rebuild the St Ebbe's community, and the street-names, Faulkner Street and Pike Terrace, were inspired by the names of lost streets. Rounding the corner into Faulkner Street, notice the prominent block of flats, Norfolk House (1998, Douglas Riach/David Shorrock), which occupies the site of the Albion pub; this was built on the Littlegate Tanyard site in c.1869, and survived into the 1970s. Near the Albion, you would often have smelled fish and chips frying at Carlo's, on the corner of Commercial Road and Blackfriars Road. Carlo Marchetti, another Italian immigrant, founded the business here in c.1900, and it operated in friendly rivalry with Del Nevo's nearby until the 1960s.

Back in Littlegate Street, you glimpse Littlegate House, formerly Holy Trinity Vicarage, over the rubble stone wall. The present building dates back to the 17th century, and may have been rebuilt after the 1644 fire. Your first sighting is the early 18th century stuccoed stone south range which has a central pedimented gable containing a round-headed window. The 17th century north range is lower, and built of ashlar stone and timber framing. Notice the wrought iron balcony to the first floor sash window on the street elevation, and the early 18th century doorway with a flat hood and scrolled brackets facing Turn Again Lane. The house was 'the residence of a genteel family' before the 1820s when its grounds

25. 8–10 Turn Again Lane

were sold off to make way for Wood and Orchard Streets, two short cul-de-sacs running down to Trill Mill Stream.

The entrance to Turn Again Lane, just outside Littlegate, marks the site of one of the three gateways into medieval Greyfriars, the others being in St Ebbe's Street, opposite Beef Lane, and in Church Street. Henry Taunt, who grew up in St Ebbe's, argued that the street was so-called because an inner gateway at the west end, apparently still surviving in the 1840s, was a barrier to wheeled traffic; a kink in the road leading to Penson's Gardens was evident until the 1960s. He also thought that a rubble stone barn-like structure on the corner of Wood Street, now lost, was a Greyfriars survival, but this may have been a later reconstruction using old materials. Turn Again Lane became Charles Street by 1866, but reverted to its original name in 1972. The street was very much on the urban fringe of post-medieval Oxford, with a row of small houses on the north side facing Trill Mill Stream and the meadows beyond.

Nos. 6–10, all 17th century in origin, faced an uncertain future in the 1950s, but Gilbert Howes, an architect, purchased no. 8 in 1954 and restored the building for family use with a grant from the City Council. The 1958 St Ebbe's plan envisaged a multi-storey car park on the site, and Howes' counter-proposal to restore the entire row did not find official favour. The City compulsorily purchased the houses in the 1960s, and demolished nos. 6–7 in 1968 during preparatory work for Westgate. After a lengthy battle, Oxford Preservation Trust acquired nos.

26. A group of Greyfriars (not shown on map)

8–10 in 1971, and successfully restored them as its new headquarters, thus conserving a picturesque fragment of old St Ebbe's. No. 10 is a two storey house with an attic dormer window; the ground floor is of rubble stone and the first floor is of rendered timber-framing. Nos. 8-9 are also two storeyed and have stuccoed fronts with large gabled attic dormers. The site of nos. 6–7 is now Greyfriars Place, a pocket park beside Westgate, but rendered council houses opposite (1987, City Architect's Office) effectively complement the retained buildings.

Medieval St Ebbe's, like the 19th century suburb, has virtually vanished but, if you walk up Roger Bacon Lane, you will find a small section of the city wall serving as the back boundary wall to nos. 8–10 Turn Again Lane. This lies close to the point where, in 1244, Henry III gave the Greyfriars permission to breach the city wall and extend their priory. The first two Franciscans, or Greyfriars, had arrived in Oxford in 1224, three years after the Blackfriars. They lodged with the Blackfriars for just eight days before renting a house in St Ebbe's and, as their numbers and popularity grew, they swiftly acquired property between Church Street and the city wall. Henry III's writ in 1244 enabled the Greyfriars to extend their precinct to Trill Mill Stream and, in 1245, he granted them the island called Boteham beyond that stream. The new Greyfriars church under construction between 1246 and 1248 filled the gap in the city defences, and the friars were also required to build a crenellated wall around their enlarged precinct.

Writing in 1892, Andrew Little could only speculate about the layout of the priory because it had been largely submerged beneath later buildings. Archaeological excavations during the construction of the original Westgate (1967–72), and the extension to the shopping centre (2015) revealed the plan of a complex which would, if it had survived, be one of Oxford's major tourist sights. The 1960s excavations concentrated on the site of the friary church which was initially a rectangular structure about 100 feet long by 30 feet wide. This soon became the choir of a much larger building as a nave and a north aisle were added to the west, and a steeple or bell-tower was presumably built between the nave and the choir. By c.1330, the north aisle had been extended northwards, almost to Church Street, to form a highly unusual north nave containing ten chapels. This feature effectively doubled the preaching and teaching area of the church, and testified to the important role which the Greyfriars played in the growth of the University in the 13th century.

The early Westgate excavations barely touched the conventual buildings of the Greyfriars which lay further south. In 2015, archaeologists were able to expose a fascinating complex of buildings enclosed within the 13th century stone precinct wall which extended south to Trill Mill Stream. These included the cloister south of the church, the kitchen and refectory, and a stone-lined water channel serving the reredorter (toilet block) adjoining the dorter (dormitory). All this has now vanished beneath the new Westgate building in Old Greyfriars Street (2015–17, Allies and Morrison), but the excavation enthused thousands with an unexpected glimpse of medieval Oxford.

The Franciscans were zealous for learning, and Agnellus of Pisa, founder of the Oxford friary, soon built a school, appointing Robert Grosseteste (c.1170–1253), a scientist and theologian, as its first lecturer in 1231. The school quickly gained an international reputation, attracting friars from across Europe, and supplying teachers to many Franciscan schools on the Continent. One of its greatest scholars was Roger Bacon (c.1219–c.1292), philosopher, linguist and founder of modern scientific method. A plaque recording the approximate site of his burial in Greyfriars church was fixed on a surviving section of city wall in 1917, and it has been relocated to the north side of Turn Again Lane just beyond Greyfriars Place; he is also remembered by Roger Bacon Lane.

Both the Blackfriars and the Greyfriars emphasized their commitment to humility and piety – indeed, this was part of their initial appeal – but their lifestyle in grand buildings became much less austere. The Greyfriars showed few signs of religious fervour by the early 16th century, and the great topographer, John Leland, found cobwebs, moths, bookworms, and a total absence of learned books in their library.

Friar Arthur was 'seen in a chamber at the sign of the Bear with a woman in a red cap ... both locked together in a chamber'. Individual friars were accused of threatening violence against the local brewer, Richard Leke, during a dispute about a garden he had leased from the Warden. Many friars had already left when Dr London arrived to dissolve the House in 1538, and he noted 'much ruinous building.' Almost to the end, however, people were leaving bequests to the Greyfriars, and a reconciled Richard Leke asked to be buried in the church in 1526, leaving money for masses to be said for his soul.

Dr London petitioned Thomas Cromwell in 1538 to secure the Blackfriars and Greyfriars sites for the town because their watercourses would provide 'convenient and commodious places to set fulling mills upon, and so people might be set to work'. Nothing came of this proposal, and most of the Greyfriars buildings were soon demolished, leaving only walls that were to serve as major property boundaries. Alderman Richard Gunter, a brewer and college servant, and his wife, Joanna, acquired the Greyfriars site in 1544, and the gradual subdivision of this large estate played a crucial role in the later history of St Ebbe's.

The unlovely Westgate multi-storey car park (1974, Ernest Ireland Ltd.) dominated the view at the end of Turn Again Lane until it was demolished in 2015. The car park was originally described as 'the most advanced in Europe' and its most interesting feature was an extraordinary geodesic dome, usually known as the golf ball, which housed control staff and equipment. The golf ball lasted until the 1990s and pedestrians making for Castle Street subsequently had little to savour in Old Greyfriars Street, then a grim defile between the shopping centre's goods entrance and the multi-storey car park. When an extension to the Westgate Centre was first proposed in 1988, this dreary route seemed likely to disappear quite quickly, but several schemes came and went before the present one was granted planning permission in 2014. Old Greyfriars Street now runs south towards Speedwell Street and Turn Again Lane has been extended through Westgate, providing a more welcoming pedestrian route to Norfolk Street where you have a distant glimpse of trees and the Castle pub. Meanwhile, you are swiftly aware of the sheer scale of the Westgate development with footbridges on two levels carrying shoppers between the refurbished 1960s arcade and the new shops. Below one of these bridges, turn left into South Arcade and left again immediately to take the lift up to the Upper Ground floor. Popping out here, notice above the lift door a display of 13th century floor tiles from the Greyfriars cloister walk that archaeologists excavated in 2015. You can then take the lift to the roof terrace or, with a greater sense of anticipation, ascend by the nearby escalator.

Motorists and the occasional urban explorer could enjoy a roof-top view towards Christ Church from the old multi-storey car park, but the Westgate roof terrace is very much higher and accessible to all. It provides stupendous views, and the glazed handrail almost suggests that you are a cruise ship passenger gazing down upon some approaching historic port. From here, you can spy elements of the walk such as St Ebbe's Church tower, the City Brewery tower, the spire of St Aldate's Church, Tom Tower and the other great Christ Church buildings, the Oxford Preservation Trust houses in Turn Again Lane and the Deaf Centre in Littlegate Street. You can perhaps conjure up images of how different the view would have been when Blackfriars flourished beyond Trill Mill Stream, when Treadwell's garden occupied that site or, later, when streets of terraced housing filled St Ebbe's. You can also indulge in flights of fancy – what if The Friars district had been retained, an urban motorway had been built across the area or the Preachers Lane development had been completed as intended with a tower block by the river? Back in the present, you will be drawn to more distant views, eastwards beyond Christ Church and the minaret of the Manzil Way mosque towards Shotover, and southwards towards Hinksey Hill and Boars Hill. These demonstrate the beauty of Oxford's green setting, which Oxford Preservation Trust has strived to protect since it was founded in 1927.

When you have seen enough, and perhaps sampled one of the adjacent bars and restaurants, take the lift or escalator down to Leiden Square, named in honour of Oxford's town-twinning link established in 1946. Walk back along South Arcade at upper ground level, and turn left into Church Lane to reach Castle Street.

5 Oxford Castle and Paradise

Castle Street was formerly 'one of the most beautiful streets in the city' with a wealth of gabled, timber-framed houses, but most had gone by the late 1960s when the 16th century stone doorway of the Paviers Arms, retained when the pub was rebuilt in the 1930s, was among the casualties. No. 29A Castle Street, across the road from Church Lane, is the only survivor of the many houses that were built in the silted-up castle moat in Castle Street and Paradise Street from the late 16th century. The left hand part may date from the late 17th century, and it is two storeyed, timber framed and rendered with a gabled dormer in the slate roof. The right hand part is early 19th century, three storeys high, and also rendered over a timber frame.

Castle Street was realigned in 1967 to make way for the Westgate Centre, and as the first phase of a major road that was to run along New Inn Hall Street to a multi-storey car park in Gloucester Green. The road scheme was abandoned, but the original Westgate Centre (1968–73, City Architect's Office/Douglas Murray) presented an almost windowless façade to Castle Street, punctuated by a series of metal ventilation shafts. The refurbished Westgate (2016–17, Dixon Jones) has added some windows and a brick tower with a glass lantern to the concrete behemoth, but the concrete and glass County Council offices (1974, County Architect's Office/Albert Smith) opposite do little to raise the spirits.

27. 29a Castle Street

Archaeological excavations and documentary research fortunately enable us to explore a street for which the above ground historical clues have largely vanished. The original Castle Street was part of the fortified burh laid out in c.900, and probably led west from today's Queen Street to a point near Quaking Bridge. The West Gate in the town's western defences would have been west of a line marked by New Inn Hall Street and St Ebbe's Street or close to St George's Tower. It is argued that the building of Oxford Castle in 1071 caused the southerly diversion of Castle Street and the removal of West Gate to its medieval position in Paradise Street. St Budoc's Church was established on the east side of Castle Street by the early 12th century, but this church and other buildings were demolished in 1215–16 when Fawkes de Breauté was holding the Castle for King John against the barons and built a defensive barbican on the site. As the strategic importance of the Castle waned, the site of the barbican was transformed by c.1420 into Newmarket, a wide market place at the lower end of Castle Street. This was presumably intended for the sale of country produce, but it was no longer in use by 1532, and the City gradually leased the surplus land for building.

Before crossing Castle Street with care, notice the half-timbered Castle pub,

28. Detail of Greyfriars cartouche, Paradise House

formerly the Paradise House (1892, H. G. W. Drinkwater), on the corner of Norfolk Street and Paradise Street which provides another opportunity for refreshment. The street-name 'Norfolk Street' has been much-travelled, originating on the Littlegate Tanyard site in the 1860s before being attached to part of the new St Ebbe's road layout in the 1960s, and then coming to rest here in the 1980s; until then, this was the east side of Paradise Square. Now walk into Paradise Street, passing on your right Simon House (1981, J. Alan Bristow & Partners), a hostel built on the site of the castle moat. The medieval West Gate stood across Paradise Street just beyond the Castle Tavern, and was pulled down soon after 1600. One account of the St Scholastica's Day riot in 1355 paints a vivid picture of 'about 2,000 countrymen, with a black dismal flag, erect and displayed' entering by the West Gate to join the fray.

On the south side of the street, Greyfriars, formerly Paradise House, now occupies part of that site. The building consists of a late 17th century main range with its gable end to the street and a three storey early 18th century block west of the garden. Only the ornate stone doorway (c.1700) with a rich foliage cartouche gives any hint of the fine wood and plaster work that survives inside the building. According to unfounded tradition, Paradise House was the one-time home of Sir Mathew Hale, one of the judges who refused to release John Bunyan from prison in 1661 after hearing a plea by the author's wife, Elizabeth. By the early 20th century, O. H. Ball could describe it as 'an old house which has fallen on evil days', and the narrator in her novel *Barbara Goes to Oxford* declares: 'you would not like the neighbourhood – there is a public house on either hand and the smell of fried fish floated on the air.' Fortunately, the building found new uses, firstly as the headquarters of the City's community health services until 1974, and then as a private tutorial college. Beyond Greyfriars, you come to a gabled timber-framed cottage which was derelict for many years before being incorporated into the adjacent Jolly Farmers public house. The pub dates from the 17th century, and is a picturesque two storey rubble stone and timber-framed structure with a north-facing gable and first floor jetty.

These buildings outside the West Gate on the south side of Paradise Street took over the site of the second St Budoc's Church. After the demolition of the original church in Castle Street, Henry III paid for a replacement church to be built here in 1223, but St Budoc's was a very poor parish, and he subsequently granted the church and associated land to the Penitential Friars or Friars of the Sack in 1265. Their alternative name derived from wearing habits made of sack-cloth; underneath, their only concession to comfort was 'a little pare of linnen drawers to save their privy members from their coarse habit'. The Penitential Friars flourished briefly but the order was suppressed in 1274, and gradually died out. Edward II granted the site to the Greyfriars in 1310, and it went on to become their Paradise, a garden outside the precinct wall which was bounded on the south by Trill Mill Stream and on the west by Castle Mill Stream. The name Paradise survived the Dissolution, applied not only to the garden but also to a house and pub, a street, and the square which you are now entering.

The low-lying site behind Paradise Street seems to have reverted to meadow by 1578, but the Paradise Garden became both a market garden and a visitor attraction during the 17th century. Its owner, Thomas Wrench (d.1714), was described as 'the best kitchen gardener in England' and, in 1725, his successor and former apprentice, Thomas Tagg, claimed a wage bill of £700 a year at this and his other Oxford market gardens. Zacharias von Uffenbach, a German visitor to Oxford in 1710, described the garden as being chiefly dedicated to cookery, but he noted also fine fruit trees and yews, and 'by the waterside ... countless little retreats, close to each other, of cropped hedge, where the Fellows drink in summer.'

Paradise Garden continued to be cultivated as a market garden until the late 1830s, well after the first flush of building in St Ebbe's. John Chaundy, a local builder, then bought the land from a later Thomas Tagg, and sold building plots at a series of auctions between 1838 and 1847. These lots were in and around what became Paradise Square but, because of the pre-existing houses in Paradise Street, there could only be building on three sides of the square. By 1850, the development was virtually complete with stuccoed three storey houses on the east side of the square, and diaper brick two and three storey ones on the south and west sides. Paradise Square never quite achieved fashionable status and, in 1851, the central area was described as 'a desert waste.' This problem was solved when St Ebbe's Rectory, a picturesque two storey stone house (1854, G. E. Street; extended 1868) was placed in the middle of the square. Notice on the north elevation a blue plaque to the Rev John Stansfeld (1854–1938), who was a much-loved rector of the parish between 1912 and 1926. He was nick-named 'The Doctor' because he was a qualified physician, and he fought tirelessly to improve conditions in St Ebbe's. His wife died in the 1918 flu epidemic and, in her memory, he bought some 20 acres of land at Shotover in 1919 to serve as a 'green lung' for St Ebbe's, building small houses where families could go for a week's holiday.

The rectory garden, still partially retained as a public open space, was a remarkable oasis in St Ebbe's. Stansfeld encouraged local volunteers to build a parish dispensary called St Budoc's Room in the garden in 1923, and he also erected a St Ebba's folly gateway which survived into the 1970s. Opposite the rectory, where the Premier Inn (2019–, Rick Mather Architects) now stands, he helped to persuade the City to build a public bath-house (1923), which provided local people with affordable hot baths and a warm meeting place. Rosemary Russell-Vines, growing up in the area in the 1940s, remembered awaiting her turn there with soap and towel, sometimes sharing a bath with one of her sisters.

Continue south along Paradise Square where the back gateway of the Rectory bears the date A.D. 1868 and a coat of arms with the motto, 'Via Crucis, Via Salutis' – the Way of the Cross, the Way of Salvation. Black brick pavements had become usual in Oxford's narrow streets by 1879 and the retained length here probably dates from the 19th century. On the stone wall beyond the rectory, notice three brackets beneath a rusty iron canopy which formerly housed a fire ladder. Such ladders were installed around Oxford from 1870 to make it easier to rescue fire victims; the possibility that burglars might use them seems not to have been considered!

Some Paradise Square houses were popular guest-houses, especially with actors on tour in the city. One former resident recalled that business was particularly brisk during the Second World War when thousands of servicemen were stationed in and around Oxford and unattached girls flocked in from as far afield as Manchester. The owner of a room-letting agency was apparently imprisoned for running a brothel in the square. After the War, Paradise Square suffered years of planning blight and, although all the houses were eventually listed, this did not save them. The writer, Brian Aldiss, a temporary resident in 1961, criticized the City's decision to destroy a strong community that was so close to Carfax and yet so secluded that children could play in the street. The last house in the square was demolished in 1972. The Westgate car park occupied the east side of the square, but three storey flats and council houses were eventually built on the west side (1981), and decent council flats (1986) on the south side; the latter were controversially pulled down for the recent Westgate development. Tennyson Lodge (1994, Oxford Architects Partnership), south of the rectory, occupied the site of St Ebbe's School (1858, G. E. Street: with many later additions), which had moved to new buildings in White House Road in 1975. The yellow brick panels of the John Lewis store now close the view at the end of Paradise Square with Mill Stream House (2015–17, Glenn Howells Associates), a four storey apartment block, away to your right. Between buses, this can be a surprisingly peaceful spot where you may even hear birdsong! Standing here, you are approximately on the line of Trill Mill Stream which formed a barrier between Paradise Square and Abbey Place. The St Ebbe's street-name Abbey Place has been adopted for the road beside Mill Stream House; the old Abbey Place, a cul-de-sac from New Street, led to Bennett's City Laundry, a major local employer of women and girls from c.1900 to 1960.

Turn right out of Paradise Square, and right again onto the footpath between Castle Mill Stream and the backs of the Paradise Square houses. Through the trees to your left, you can enjoy the view at the point where Castle Mill Stream and Wareham Stream, two branches of the River Thames, merge and flow on towards the main river. A sluice gate at this point marks the beginning of the Trill Mill Stream, now diverted around Westgate basements before it eventually emerges into the light in Christ Church Memorial Garden. You pass a timber footbridge decorated with metal swallows, an art installation (2009, Jon Mills) created as part of the nearby Empress Court development in Woodin's Way (2005, PRP Architects). The bridge provides a splendid view of St George's Tower and Oxford Castle motte or mound. Notice to the right of the footbridge, a rubble stone building with a slate roof (c.1810) which formed part of a malthouse complex associated with the former Swan Brewery across Castle Mill Stream; a persistent survivor, it was converted into three flats in 2015. Continue past this building and Swan Court (1994, McDermott Associates) to reach Paradise Street.

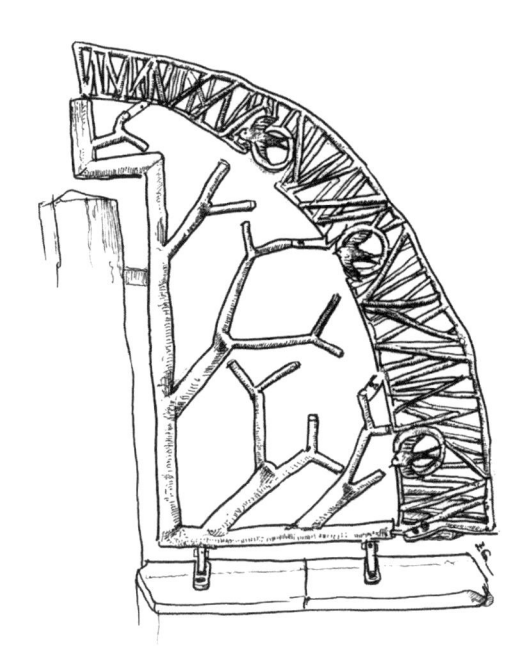

29. Metal swallows on timber footbridge near Empress Court

You emerge just a few paces west of the entrance to Paradise Square with views towards Westgate away to your right. To your left, student accommodation for St Peter's College (2003, Anthony Rickett Partnership) occupied part of the castle moat that was a City Waterworks depot for much of the 20th century. Straight across Paradise Street, you can now enter Oxford Castle through Gate 3, a breach in the late 18th century prison wall, and explore the previously forbidden site which was successfully restored and redeveloped by Trevor Osborne Property Group and Oxfordshire County Council (2004–6). Oxford Castle was a motte (mound) and bailey castle built by Robert d'Oilly in 1071, just five years after the Norman Conquest, but it seems likely that there was already an administrative centre on part of the site. Away to your left, St George's Tower has traditionally been dated to the founding or re-founding of the Church of St George's in the Castle in 1074, but it is now thought to have been built in c.1020 as a watchtower strengthening the town's western approaches. The door in the north-east corner of the tower is associated with the famous episode during King Stephen's siege of the Empress Matilda in December 1142 when she escaped over the wall during a snowstorm, dressed in white, and made her way to Wallingford.

The Castle was used as a gaol as early as the 12th century and it retained that function for centuries. During the Civil War, the Castle was garrisoned by the

30. Empress Matilda's door in St George's Tower

Royalists and Parliamentary prisoners were housed there in unhealthy conditions that were blamed on Smith, the gaoler. Prisoners were housed in St George's Tower and in an adjoining building where John Wesley, founder of the Methodist movement, visited and ministered to them in 1738. The prison reformer, John Howard, criticized this small, overcrowded and verminous prison in 1777. You are now standing just inside the County Gaol built by the county magistrates between 1785 and 1805 under the supervision of William Blackburn, the pioneering prison designer. Initially, it comprised a felons' wing, a debtors' wing, and Houses of Correction. The felons' wing (c.1785), later known as C Wing, is the three storey stone building directly in front of you which had to be substantially rebuilt (2004–6) because the two upper storeys were removed during the 20th century; you can, however, visit some cheerless work cells on the ground floor if you walk round to the left of the circular tower base. They were traditionally known as the Wesley cells, but they long post-date his visits. The Houses of Correction (c.1788) are away to your left, one for males and one for females. They are two rectangular blocks of coursed rubble stone with stone quoins and dressings. A modern linking block has replaced the Keeper's House that originally stood between them. The two storey debtors' wing (c.1795–1805, William Blackburn & Daniel Harris) is at the far end of the lawn, attached to St George's Tower. This range, later known as D Wing, originally had a vaulted ground floor which was partially open to the outside to improve air circulation; an

31. King Stephen and Empress Matilda puppets (not shown on map)

external balcony gave access to part of the first floor on this side of the building. The circular debtors' tower, furthest from St George's Tower, retains its original cell doors and partitions. Prisoners erected all these buildings under the watchful eye of their gaoler, Daniel Harris (c.1760–1840), who was also a builder, civil engineer and architect. He had strong archaeological interests, and ensured that the Norman capitals from the crypt of St George's Church were rebuilt in an atmospheric crypt beneath D Wing.

The County Gaol had become too small by the 1840s, and the complex you see now was completed when A Wing (1852–6, H. J. Underwood & J. C. Buckler) provided 150 additional cells between the two earlier wings. The building is of coursed rubble with stone dressings, and three storeys high above a semi-basement; notice the drainpipes sunk in the walls to deter escapers. Internally, A Wing followed the 'separate' system pioneered at Pentonville where prisoners in solitary confinement could reflect on the consequences of their crimes. The closure of Oxford Prison, first suggested in 1946, led to the brilliant, if improbable, conversion of these premises into luxury hotel accommodation (2004–6, Architects Design Partnership with Jestico & White). Every three cells in A Wing became a double bedroom and bathroom, and the continuous sill bands of the upper floor windows were retained when new windows were inserted to light these rooms.

Returning to Gate 3, walk up the ramp between the former C Wing and apartments built on the site of temporary prison buildings. Excavations here in 2003 traced a section of the Saxon ramparts, and a display shows views inside and outside the town wall in c.1050. At the top of the ramp, you come to the gable end of A Wing which has large windows lighting the internal atrium and the galleries to the cells. A stone plaque on the wall records the official opening of Oxford Castle by Queen Elizabeth II on May 5th, 2006. The stone-built 19th century Governor's Office beside A Wing had been retained as part of the prison laundry, but other prison buildings in this area had already been cleared. They included the former women's prison (B Wing) (1849, H. J. Underwood) at the north-east corner of the site which showed clear signs of subsiding into the castle moat before it was demolished in c.1979.

Leave the Castle by Gate 4, which is approximately on the site of the medieval barbican and a later toll road through the Castle that was used until c.1834. The Swan and Castle on the left takes its name from one of the many lost pubs in this area and, walking back up Castle Street towards Bonn Square, you may also like to recall other vanished features. The former bath-house on the corner of Bath Court, a cut-through to New Road and Bulwarks Lane, had perhaps the most unusual history. Built in 1852, it ceased to be used as a bath-house, and became a workshop after the boiler exploded in 1865. In 1910, the building was converted to become the City's first dedicated cinema known as the Oxford Electric Theatre, or, more usually, the Castle Street Theatre. Competition from more modern cinemas led to closure in c.1923, but the building had a lengthy after-life as a council canteen before it was demolished in 1968. Macfisheries Corner on the corner of New Road and Castle Street also occupied a prominent place in the memories of many Oxonians. Rosemary Russell-Vines recalled that 'they had a tiled pool under the slabs where live fish swam, it was always a place to take littl'uns to see the fishes while you were shopping.'

Once back in Bonn Square, walk back along Queen Street towards Carfax, enjoying the distant view of the former All Saints' Church (1706–9, Henry Aldrich; steeple 1718–20 by Aldrich and Nicholas Hawksmoor). Nearing Carfax, you can also appreciate the amazingly flamboyant Lloyds Bank building (1900–3, Davey & Salter) across the road. The delightful ship weathervane on the corner turret is a reference to Lloyds' maritime origins.

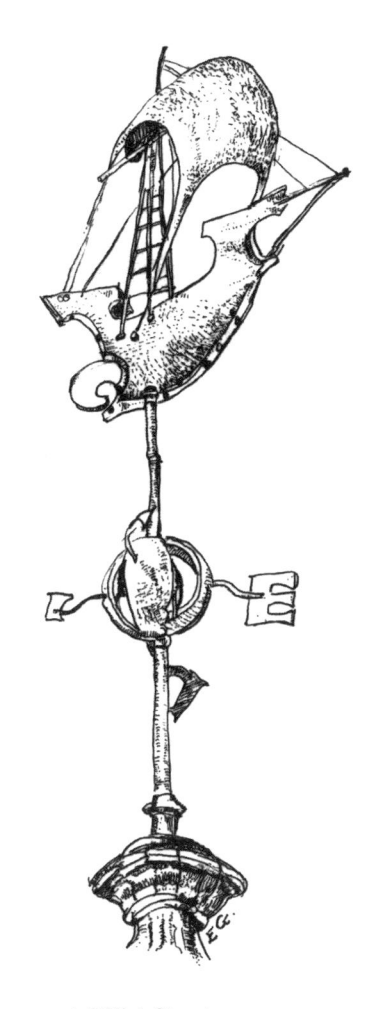

32. Lloyds Bank weathervane, 1–3 High Street

Notes and Further Reading

H. W. Acland, *Memoir on the Cholera at Oxford in 1854* (1856)

Barclay Baron, *The Doctor; the Story of John Stansfeld of Oxford and Bermondsey* (1952)

Paul Booth, The west gate of Oxford Castle, *Oxoniensia* 68 (2003)

British Industries Business Review (1895)

M. J. H. Bunney & C. M. Pearce, *An Oxford Survey* (1935)

Barbara Burke [O. H. Ball], *Barbara Goes to Oxford* (1907)

J. I. Catto, ed., *The History of the University of Oxford, vol. 1: the Early Oxford Schools* (1984)

Andrew Clark, ed., Survey of the Antiquities of the City of Oxford, by Anthony Wood, vol. 1, *Oxford Historical Society* 15 (1889)

Andrew Clark, ed., Survey of the Antiquities of the City of Oxford, by Anthony Wood, vol. 2, *Oxford Historical Society* 17 (1890)

Annual Reports of the Medical Officer of Health of the City of Oxford

Edmund Chillenden, *The inhumanity of the King's Prison-Keeper at Oxford* (1643)

Catherine Cole, Carfax Conduit, *Oxoniensia* 29/30 (1964/5)

H. M. Colvin, The architects of All Saints' Church, *Oxoniensia* 19 (1954)

G. V. Cox, *Recollections of Oxford* (1868)

Alan Crossley, ed., *Victoria History of the County of Oxford, vol. 4: the City of Oxford* (1979)

Reg Crossley, *Planning Policies in Jericho and St Ebbe's from 1919* (1975)

Judith Curthoys, *The Cardinal's College: Christ Church, Chapter and Verse* (2012)

Judith Curthoys, 'To Perfect the College…', the Christ Church Almsmen, 1546-1888, *Oxoniensia* 60 (1995)

Mark Davies and Catherine Robinson, *A Towpath Walk in Oxford* (2003)

Anne Dodd, *Oxford Before the University* (2003)

Richard Foster, *F. Cape & Co* (1973)

C.E. Goad Ltd., Oxford, Oxfordshire [Shopping Centre Maps]

Malcolm Graham, *Diverse Oxfordshire* (2010)

Malcolm Graham, *Henry Taunt of Oxford: Victorian Photographer* (1973)

Malcolm Graham, *Oxford in the Great War* (2014)

Malcolm Graham, The building of Oxford Covered Market, *Oxoniensia* 46 (1979)

Claire Halpin, Late Saxon Evidence and Excavation of Hinxey Hall, Queen Street, Oxford, *Oxoniensia* 48 (1983)

T. G. Hassall, *Oxford Beneath Your Feet* (1972)

T. G. Hassall, C.E. Halpin and M. Mellor, Excavations in St Ebbe's, Oxford: Part II, Post-Medieval Domestic Tenements, and the Post-Medieval Site of the Greyfriars, *Oxoniensia* 49 (1984)

Christopher Hibbert, *The Encyclopaedia of Oxford* (1988)

M. G. Hobson and H. E. Salter, *Oxford Council Acts, 1626-1665* (1933)

R. S. Hoggar, *Map of Oxford* (1850)

Peter Howell, Oxford Architecture, 1800-1914, In, M.G. Brock and M.C. Curthoys, eds., *History of the University of Oxford, vol. 7: 19th Century Oxford, Part 2* (2000)

Hunt's Oxford Dircctory (1846)

Herbert Hurst, Oxford Topography: an Essay, *Oxford Historical Society* 39 (1899)

Kelly's Directory of Oxford, Abingdon, Woodstock and Neighbourhood

George Lambrick & Humphrey Woods, Excavations on the Second Site of the Dominican Priory, Oxford, *Oxoniensia* 41 (1976)

A. G. Little, The Grey Friars in Oxford, *Oxford Historical Society* 20 (1892)

P. J. Marriott, *Early Oxford Picture Palaces* (1978)

P. J. Marriott, *Oxford Pubs Past & Present* (1978)

Ministry of Housing & Local Government, *Supplementary List of Buildings of Architectural or Historic Intererest: City of Oxford* (1954?)

Henry Minn, *South-West Ward* (Bodleian Library MS. Top. Oxon. d.492)

Henry Minn, *St. Aldate's* (Bodleian Library MS. Top. Oxon. d.503)

J. M. Mogey, *Family and Neighbourhood: Two Studies in Oxford* (1956)

John Moore, St Ebbe's Church, *Oxoniensia* 69 (2004)

R. J. Morris, The Friars and Paradise: an Essay in the Building History of Oxford, 1801-1861, *Oxoniensia* 36 (1971)

Julian Munby, *Oxford Castle Medieval and Later Buildings* (2000)

Julian Munby, Zacharias's: a 14th Century Oxford New Inn and the Origins of the Medieval Urban Inn, *Oxoniensia* 57 (1992)

James Neild, *State of the Prisons in England, Scotland and Wales...* (1812)

Carol Newbigging, *Changing Faces of St Ebbe's and St Thomas's, Book 1* (1997)

Carol Newbigging, *Changing Faces of St Ebbe's and St Thomas's, Book 2* (1997)

Philip Opher, *Pocket Guide to Twentieth Century Oxford Architecture* (1995)

Oxford Archaeology, *Archaeological Excavations: the Greyfriars Buildings* (2015)

Oxford Archaeology, *Oxford Castle: a Heritage Survey* (1996)

Oxford City Council, *Council Reports*

Oxford City Council, *Planning Applications*

Oxford Preservation Trust, *Annual Reports*

Oxfordshire Buildings Record 147, 84 St Aldate's, Oxford (2012)

William Page, ed., *Victoria History of the County of Oxford, vol. 2* (1907)

Harry Paintin, *Articles on Oxford and District* (c.1930)

W. A. Pantin, *Oxford Life in Oxford Archives* (1972)

Andy Panton, *Farewell St Ebbe's* (1980)

W. T. Pike, *Views & Reviews Special Edition Oxford* (1897)

Stephen Porter, The Oxford Fire of 1644, *Oxoniensia* 49 (1984)

W. H. & W. J. C. Quarrell, eds., *Oxford in 1710, from the Travels of Zacharias Conrad von Uffenbach* (1928)

Penelope Renold, *St Aldate's, Oxford, Parish Register Transcripts* (1989)

A Report...into the State of the Sewerage, Drainage and Water Supply of the University and City of Oxford (1851)

J. S. Reynolds, *Canon Christopher of St Aldate's, Oxford* (1967)

John Rhodes, *Oxford Castle Conservation Plan* (1999)

Cecil Roth, The Jews of Medieval Oxford, *Oxford Historical Society New Series* 9 (1951)

Royal Commission on Historical Monuments England, *An Inventory of the Historical Monuments in the City of Oxford* (1939)

Rosemary Russell-Vines, *Growing Up in St Ebbe's, 1941-1959* (2008)

H. E. Salter, Medieval Oxford, *Oxford Historical Society* 100 (1936)

H. E. Salter, Munimenta Civitas Oxonie, *Oxford Historical Society* 71 (1920)

H. E. Salter, *Oxford City Properties* (1926)

H. E. Salter, Survey of Oxford volume 2, *Oxford Historical Society New Series* 20 (1969)

Jennifer Sherwood and Nikolaus Pevsner, *Oxfordshire* (1974)

T. W. Squires, *In West Oxford* (1928)

David Sturdy, Houses of the Oxford Region, *Oxoniensia* 26/27 (1961/2)

David Sturdy, *Twelve Oxford Gardens* (198-)

David Sturdy and Julian Munby, Early Domestic Sites in Oxford: Excavations in Cornmarket and Queen Street, 1959-62, *Oxoniensia* 50 (1985)

Victor Sugden, *An Oxford Diary* (2009)

Ann Spokes Symonds and Nigel Morgan, *The Origins of Oxford Street Names* (2010)

Margaret Toynbee and Peter Young, *Strangers in Oxford* (1973),

Richard Tyler, Archaeological Investigations during the Refurbishment of St Aldate's Church, Oxford, *Oxoniensia* 66 (2001)

W. M. Wade, *Walks in Oxford*, 2nd ed (1818)

John Walker, *Oxoniana, vol. 1* (1809)

E. J. Warr, *The Oxford Plaque Guide* (2011)

Edward Wirley, *The Prisoner's report* (1642)

Anthony Wood, *Ancient and Present State of the City of Oxford...with additions by the Rev Sir J. Peshall* (1773)

A. R. Woolley, *The Clarendon Guide to Oxford* (1963)

Liz Woolley, Industrial Architecture in Oxford, 1870-1914, *Oxoniensia* 75 (2010)

http://www.cpreoxon.org.uk/news/news-archive/item/2209-oxpens-meadow
https://www.cwgc.org/find/find-war-dead

http://oti.eng.ox.ac.uk/about/history/
http://www.fieldsintrust.org/FieldSite/Oxpens-Meadow
https://www.freebmd.org.uk/
https://www.heritagegateway.org.uk
https://historicengland.org.uk/images-books/photos/
https://historicengland.org.uk/images-books/archive/collections/
https://www.npg.org.uk/collections/
https://www.bodleian.ox.ac.uk/oua
https://www.oxford.gov.uk/downloads/download/153/oxpens masterplan spd
https://www.oxforddnb.com/
http://www.oxfordhistory.org.uk/
http://www.oxfordshireblueplaques.org.uk/
http://www.stsepulchres.org.uk/
https://www.thisisoxfordshire.co.uk/

https://www.bnc.ox.ac.uk/
http://www.marcus-beale.com/
https://www.prp-co.uk/
https://www.spc.ox.ac.uk/
https://www.wikipedia.org/

A fully referenced copy of the text of this Oxford Heritage Walk can be viewed at www.oxfordpreservation.org.uk